From God's Lips to My Ears

By Charr Leslie

Charr Leslie Publishers
CharrLeslie@yahoo.com

For Worldwide Distribution, Published in the U.S.A.

ISBN 13: 978-0-615-29808-5

Book Design Copyright 2009 by Charr Leslie Publishing
All Rights Reserved
Cover Design by Joe Mandeville
Edited by Jima Dunigan

For contact information:
CharrLeslie@yahoo.com

About the Author, Charr Leslie

In the Bible, names often personified the person, the person fulfilled the prophecy of his or her name, or the name began to represent a certain characteristic from the life of that person. That phenomenon fits the author of this book.

Charr says a seasoned prophet of God in Tennessee prophesied and prayed over her, again and again, saying, "Charlotte, you will take your torch light into dark places." One day, she looked up the meaning of her name. She discovered that her name, Charlotte, means "little woman" and Ellen means "with a torch light." Charr is a petite woman, under five feet tall. The torch light she bears is the light and sword of God that is faithful and true, never failing, and constant. Amazing how God named her at birth, both regarding her size and her calling.

As a young woman, she accepted Jesus Christ as her personal Savior and soon God called her to the ministry. He began to use her to teach the Word of God, sing, and flow in the Gifts of the Holy Spirit. She has traveled widely over the years, and is well loved by those to whom she has brought the Lord's ministry to their lives.

Through tragedies and sorrows, Charr held on to God, knowing he was her only hope. During a particular time of darkness in her own life, when dark circumstances surrounded her and left her nearly despairing of life, again, Charr bowed before God, out of this time of darkness, God called her to sit still before Him and listen. In obedience to God's direction, Charr began writing the beautiful words God whispered to her heart. What she did not know at the time, was that God was opening a new avenue, a new door, from which more people would be blessed. As she shared the words of hope and encouragement from her time with God, friends wanted to also share those words with others, and through this, Charr began her book ministry.

Hurting people, especially women, anywhere can read and be encouraged, be healed, and develop a more personal relationship with an Almighty living God, our Father. Godly women can learn to become a "Woman with a Torch Light."

Introduction

Dear Readers,

I pray that as you journey with me through this particularly difficult time of my life, that you will find answers to questions you may have regarding your present circumstances.

Our Heavenly Father brought me through those trying times, and because he does the same thing for us all, he will help you too.

Be encouraged that he loves you, and wants the very best for you. Put your trust in the Lord right now, and allow him to touch everything in your life that needs his touch.
You will arise from the ashes and see beauty again, trust me; I know because I have seen the ashes of my life, transformed into beauty. He will do it for you as well.

I have included a prayer after each journal entry, I am hoping this will help you in your communication with the Father.

I would like to thank the many close Christian friends and family throughout the country that prayed for me during the time of this writing. You prayed for me; spoke the Word, and you believed that God had a purpose for my life. I will never forget the gatherings for prayer and encouragement of these my dear friends. Words could never tell of the thankfulness that fills my heart as I think of you.

Special blessings I send to "The Wrecking Crew."

I am praying that God will use this book to help people that are hurting. This is my purpose in publishing this work.

Love you,
Charr

Hearing My Voice

Daughter,

Hearing from me, hearing my voice is not such a hard thing to do. I live inside of you, near enough to speak, and you can hear what I say. This takes a settling, a slowing down and getting quiet -- then starts the hearing.

I yearn to give information and counsel to my children. They can save themselves many troubles if the art of hearing has been developed.

Today you turned a corner. Your hand has been firmly placed in mine. I am close to you to comfort and guide you. Snuggle up close, feel the warmth of my presence and hear my quiet voice as I speak to you. I have not given up on you, nor forgotten the promises made to you. Fear nothing for I am by your side, and I will protect and keep you.

Be still and know that I am God, I am a mighty God, one who delivers my loved ones. Rest and receive my comfort.

I want you to know me for yourself. When you tell others of my attributes, I want it to be from your own experiences and not learned second handed. Let me minister my ways to you.

Lovingly,
Your Faithful Father

Dear Faithful Father,

Father thank you that I can hear you speaking to me. You are within my heart and you are as close as the air I breathe. I am quieting myself so that I can hear well. It is the still small voice that I want to hear speaking to me. I thank you for the advice and counsel that you give.

Your hand leads and guides me on the path I need to walk. I thank you for your comfort and protection. I draw close to you today. Thank you that not only do you deliver me, but you are always thinking of the welfare of my family.

I invite you to reveal yourself to me personally, second hand testimonies are good, but I want to have first hand knowledge of your power and your love for me.

I receive your ministry today.

I pray and receive in Jesus' name,

Your Hearing Daughter

Choose a Time

Daughter,

I would like you to choose a time each day to come before me in prayer. As you do this, listen intently for the voice of my Spirit. He will prompt you to pray specifically on matters that He wishes to change with his touch. He will guide your heart and mind about those things I would lead you to pray about.

Bring your journal with you and record what I say to you. You must begin to look for my miracles. They are carefully placed along your pathway. I have placed fire deep within you and as you open your mouth my fire will race out and devour all your enemies. Know that I am on your side. I am for you and not against you! A lesson you are now learning is your utter dependence upon my grace. You may feel that you are the more vulnerable than you have ever been, but in truth, you are the most secure because you are in my hands, in my place, and in my time.

Your enemy would love for you to snatch a bite of an apple that I have not wanted you to bite into. He offers, but then he withdraws the offer, leaving you hurt, bitter, and disappointed. Anything I give is eternal and everlasting. I will allow your spirit to respond when something is of me. Listen to your spirit. The spirit of man receives what is of me.

Shrink back no more. I see your broken places and long to make things new again in your life. The discouragement you feel is having a profound effect upon your life. Your perceptions are clouded and jaded. Come to me for clarity.

> Encouragingly,
> Your Waiting Father

Dear Waiting Father,

It is my desire to spend time in your presence. I hear your voice and a stranger's voice I rebuke in Jesus' name.

Thank you for showing me how to pray specifically. I want to target my prayers so lives can be changed for the good.

I will write about our time together; and record the things you speak to my heart. I will wait to see you move to conquer my enemies. With every step I take, I keep my eyes wide open and I will see my enemy's defeat.

Thank you for the fire that is deep within my spirit, your Spirit anoints my words, and they will act as a flamethrower to devour the spirits of the devil.

What a wonderful feeling to know that you fight for me and that you are always standing by my side.

My mouth will not bite into the devils sour apples, for my heart is seasoned with your grace. I will come to you in prayer for everything and about everything.

Thank you for resting your Spirit upon me. I am yours. I will be bold to admit my brokenness to you. Please heal the broken places, making me new again.

I refuse discouragement. I listen to and believe your promises. I confess you with my mouth.

Create in me a new heart and mind. Your Word says that I have the mind of Christ. Thank you.

In Jesus' name I Pray,

Expectantly,
Your awaiting daughter

Hosea 10:12…..for it is time to seek the Lord.

Our Time Together

Daughter,

Tell your enemies, "This is where the Lord has me right now, but I shall arise from these ashes and blaze again for his glory! I shall be placed high upon a rock, out of the reach of all my enemies!"

There is a door that will swing wide open for you. Let your light shine brightly as I bring you to the forefront in the things I have called you to do.

You will be glad you waited as I begin to reveal my plans for you. For I love you and want to bless your life. Be watchful of your words, for I anoint them. Be wise. Everything that happens in a person's life is not just about them. I have people that I want touched through you.

Your candle is flickering, but it has not gone out. I will fan it once again and you shall stand upon the victor's platform. Comfort yourself with these words, for I will move in your life and show you my great salvation and deliverance.

My timing is perfect. I am never early and I am never late. Man does not see the whole picture, nor does he see that my work is fruitful in many arenas at the same time.

Remember everything is in my time. Don't squirm to be out of your circumstances before the appointed time. Wait, I say, wait. I will bring you out with a parade.

I am your solution. Let me handle these things with my perfect timing.

Your Loving Father

Dear Loving Father,

I thank you for our time together. Thank you for choosing me to do wonderful tasks for you. I will listen for that still, small voice. Thank you that in my despair, you bring hope and promise.

Thank you for making beauty of the ashes of my life. Thank you that out of my ashes, others can also be helped. Thank you for the word to my heart for encouragement. My spirit receives the things that you give; it knows when you are speaking. Give me courage to do the things you call me to do.

My dependence is entirely upon your grace and mercy, I shrink back no more, for I need total and complete healing of the broken places of my life. I run to my rock and my fortress, and I am safe.

Thank you for renewing my courage, and thank you for giving clarity of mind to me. In the past, I was always on my mind, but I know it can't always be about me. It is about you, and about those who are in need of you.

My acquaintances see me as down, but I shall arise from this ash heap and proclaim the goodness of the Lord in the land of the living. Your anointing is shining upon me and I am burning bright with the good news of the gospel.

I know you are taking me through the fire, not around it, but I envision the victory parade. Thank you for solutions, for you are my solution. Please handle my problems in this life.

In Jesus' name I pray,

> Thankfully,
> Your Risen Daughter

Acts 3:19.....when the times of refreshing shall come from the presence of the Lord.

Focus On Me

Daughter,

Through discernment and wisdom, you recognize that I have distanced you from some of your friends. This will only be for a season. I want your total focus to be upon me. No more looking to others for help and comfort. I want to give you the help and comfort you seek.

As I speak to you through this prophetic gifting, I will not rewrite the Holy Scriptures, but give clear insight into the principles contained therein.

Again I say, "I want your eyes upon me, I want to direct you without the interference of outside influences. You are mine, bought and paid for; you are my very own. Let this knowledge sink deep within your soul."

Listen carefully to what I instruct you to do. I have a plan. Let my Spirit finish this work in you. Receive this temporary separation from friends. It is coming from my hand. This is a necessary part of your training.

Do not fear living conditions or circumstances. I can bless you with resources in a moment of time. The devil is a liar. What I give is always abundance, not scarcity. I know things are difficult for you right now, but I want you to know that these times have not taken me by surprise. Remember I have a plan!

I want to bring peace and safety to your life and I will do it. It will not be in the way that man thinks is necessary, but I will bring it about in my way and it will be with happiness for you.

Loving Father

Dear Loving Father,

I now realize that I have needed to shift my focus and look to you for help and support. Your comfort and strength is what I must have.

Father, I thank you for friends and family and for their love and concern, but now my eyes must stay fixed upon you. I belong to you; I have been paid for in full. It is amazing to ponder our relationship. My ears are open to hear what you are saying to me. Thank you for your good plan for my life. I receive this training of less dependency upon others, and more upon you.

Thank you for providing for my needs. I receive your split-second blessings. Thank you for teaching me that you always bless with abundance, and not lack. It is a relief for me to know that my Heavenly Father doesn't miss a thing. You are my Father that never sleeps or slumbers. Thank you for loving me so much, and for wanting the best for me.

I receive the safety and peace you have promised. I thank you that your way is always excellent and far surpasses the ideas of the carnal mind.

Happiness is something I have desired. I thank you for the desires of my heart.

In Jesus' name I pray,

Always,
Dependent Daughter

Psalms 9:10....And they who know your name will put their trust in you; for you Lord have not forsaken the ones who seek you.

Exciting Times

Daughter,

These can be the most exciting, productive, and fruitful times of your life.

The world sees you, and thinks you are down. When you are down that is the time to look up. When you look up, you see my face. When you look to my face and not at your problems, then, I will come and bring deliverance.

Begin to expect the season to change. I bring about the seasons. I created them. I also bring about change in one's life. This is my gift to you, my best plan for your life. Good times are ahead, look for and notice my miracles that are all around you.

Your enemy threatens and bullies, but he lacks the resources to carry out his plans. In all of this, I am making you trust me with all your heart. I am creating a true soldier in my army.

Be strong and courageous. Take your stand and refuse to budge! The enemies that tried surrounding you will all fall as I stand to fight your battles.

Let me display my glory in you. I am preparing a great move of my Spirit through your life. Use my gifting wisely and treat it with respect.

With loving care,
Your Wise Father

Dear Wise Father,

I thank you that even in times of crisis I can produce good fruit. Seasons of life come and go. I hear you say that a new season is approaching. Show me all you have planned for this new time in my life.

Thank you for the gift of life, I receive your plan for this new season. I know there are good times ahead; I see the miracles as they near my dwelling.

I will not be intimidated by the threats of the enemy; he is a defeated foe. I trust the lord with all of my heart. I receive the courage and boldness that only you can give. I stand in Jesus' name and refuse to move from the place I now stand. You are my Heavenly Warrior God. You fight for me and always win.

Father, use me however you wish, let your Spirit flow like a river through my life. Lord I respect the wonderful gifts of the Holy Spirit, and receive your wisdom in the manner I should move in them.

In Jesus' name I pray,

In waiting,
Your Productive Daughter

Psalms 5:12 For You, LORD, will bless me and cover me with your shield.

Battling Discouragement

Dear Discouraged Daughter,

It's been a season since we talked like this. I know your discouragement. The enemy tells you it's no use to try. Just know I still have control over everything in your life.

Square your shoulders and break forth with singing because I am in control. You may not understand why things happen as they do, but I know it all.

Be sensitive to my Spirit and I will show you the best road to take. Soon you will lay down your burdens. There are things that have tried to hold you in the land of familiar, but I say to you that a release is coming and when it does, it will shake loose everything that tries holding you back. I have seen you struggling to get free.

I am in your corner, longing to see you flowing in the grace I have placed within you. My word will command everything to fall off and you shall go free. I want you free, my freedom is available to all of my children. I have more for you. Let me love all of the hurts away and give you new direction and a new life full of power and promise.

Relax and release; I will show you a better way. Don't stress about family members, my help will also reach to them. Leave it all in my capable hands. I will do what is best for all of you.

With great love,
Your In-Control Father

Dear In-Control Father,

I thank you for showing me what my adversary is up to. He says I lose. You say I win. I choose to believe you. I believe you have control over what happens in my life.

My strength has returned, my shoulders are back where they belong, and I have broken free of oppression and now sing with your joy. I receive your direction, only going in the way that I sense your Spirit is directing.

Thank you for this release, I lay down, my burdens, and cast the whole of my cares upon you. This release is allowing me to leave familiar patterns, and become conformed into your image.

Thank you for the freedom to flow in your grace. I receive the deliverance you have spoken to me.

I believe you do have more of everything to give to your children. Thank you for filling my life to the fullest.

I receive your love and I thank you that it heals all of my hurt and pain. I give you my family members, thank you for giving them understanding of the things you are doing in us.

Thank you for your best for all of us.

In Jesus' name I pray,

Your Informed Daughter

Psalms 8:9 O LORD, our LORD, Your name is excellent in all the earth!

Exquisite Giftings

Dear Gifted Daughter,

Stir up the exquisite gifting of the Holy Spirit that I have placed within you! Much awaits you as you fan the flame of God and wear the mantle I have placed upon your shoulders. It is yours to wear, not for another. In these last days, I will do remarkable miracles. These miracles are to attract hearts back to me. As you are called to go out, allow free rein for my Spirit to flow. This is where you are called. I want you very familiar with the workings of my Spirit.

It will only take one major miracle for the word to get out that there is a supernatural wind of God blowing across the land. Word will spread, and my glory will fall upon the people. Never underestimate my power. I am not limited in anything I do. Excess is what I possess, not lack.

Stretch to believe me for more, it is yours for the asking. This is what you are called for. I want you known as a woman who flows in the Spirit of God! Hold out your hands to me today, for I am your God. I have called you. I send you forth, and I will go before you. I will allow you to demonstrate myself through you.

Walking in my fullness is a wonderful place to be. I desire to fill your life with good things. Trust me with your life. I am the creator of life and I hold all things in my hands, great and small.

I hold this world by my might and power. I hold you safely and securely in my hand as well.

As long as you want to be under my watchful care, you have nothing to fear. There will be times of testing by the enemy, but I always prevail, and I will strengthen and establish you throughout your lifetime.

Watchfully,
Your Prevailing Father

My Prevailing Father,

In the name of Jesus, I stir up the gifts of the Holy Spirit that you have placed within me. I fan the flame of God with my faith, and wear the mantle that you have placed upon my shoulders. Thank you for the remarkable miracles that you are pouring out to attract hearts back to you.

I yield myself to the Holy Spirit, and submit myself to his leadership and direction. I allow the Holy Spirit to reveal himself to me. I am taking notes on everything he says and does in my life.

Thank you for major miracles, for those explosions of Almightiness! You are the potter; I yield myself like clay. I allow you to make me into a vessel of your choosing. I will believe and trust you for more of your power and presence. My hands are outstretched to you, so use me to bless others.

Thank you for deeper revelation and more anointing to do your works. Thank you for this wonderful place of walking with you, knowing you in your power and love. You are a mighty God; I will fear no evil for you are my strong tower. I thank you for your watchful eye that continually rests upon me.

In the times of testing, I will trust in your unfailing love for me. You have never failed or disappointed me. Thank you for the strength that you give to me and for establishing me in the things of the Lord.

In Jesus' name I pray,

Expectantly,
Your Daughter Who Flows
In the Spirit Of God

2 Kings 2:14 And Elisha took Elijah's mantle and smote the waters....and the waters parted.

Rebuilding Your Life

Precious Daughter,

Dear one, I am in the process of rebuilding your life. Life is not always fair. I know this thing you are now going through has been a ripping of your heart, almost more than you can bear. I have strengthened you, sent help your way, and I am working on your behalf on the other end of this thing. My Angel clean-up crew is busy repairing the railway tracks where you were traveling. Things will get better in time.

Do not fear what others say. You must please me. Listen to my voice speaking to your spirit. Trust will come as I show to you my faithfulness. Grace will be supplied to you in abundance. I am able to show you everything about everything. Allow me to disperse what I deem is healthy and necessary.

I would not have you spinning and turning, I want you to have clarity of thought and have clear directions to the plans and purposes for your life. Much confusion has tried camping at your doorstep. Rid yourself of this confusion and seek my peace.

I have just pressed my thumb on the time clock for your new race. See how fast you can run. I have a blue ribbon waiting for you in the winner's circle.

I have trained you well, you were trained to win and I am well able to give you my victory.

Open your arms wide and be alert to receive all that I bring into your life. I have so many resources, too many for your mind to comprehend.

Patiently,
Your Purposeful Father

Dear Purposeful Father,

Thank you for the rebuilding. Even though I have experienced unfair things in my life, I am grateful that you gather the broken pieces and make me new again.

I really have an unfair advantage over the enemy of my soul. Your angels excel in strength and always minister to those born again of your Spirit. We are the heirs of your heavenly blessings.

Nothing can stop me because greater are you within me than the one who tries to come against me. Thank you for better days ahead.

I listen to your voice. My trust in your Word to me is growing daily. Thank you for grace and faithfulness.

I receive clarity of thought and receive your clear directions for the decisions of life. In Jesus' name I resist the enemy of confusion, and receive God's peace.

Lord I am making the turn and racing toward the finish line, I run to win, not just running aimlessly all over the track. I plan to win your blue ribbon of victory! Thank you for staying with me. You didn't give up on me and for that I am extremely thankful.

My arms are open to receive all that you have for me, and I am alert to your many resources coming my way.

I pray in Jesus' name,

Thankfully,
Your Trained Daughter

Psalms 16:11 LORD, you will show me the path of life and in Your presence is complete joy

Let It Flow

My Child, My Daughter,

Just say, "Lord, let it flow," and abundance will be yours. I am able to do the abundant thing, the more than enough, pressed down, shaken down, and running over thing! Get ready for increase! There will be an increase in ministry, increase in anointing, increase in finances, and an increase in answered prayer.

I have watched as you have struggled with the recent blow from the enemy, and I have seen how you are trying with sincerity to walk pleasing to my eyes. You need to guard your heart; some people will wound you. I will show you those who are trustworthy.

Work on your attitude about those that have caused you pain. My dealings are not always seen with the naked eye or in a time period or manner that you would notice. Remember that I keep the books, and the books have been opened and my heart is grieved at your mistreatment. Rest and be assured that I have not forgotten. Call to me throughout the day and I will be a strong presence in your life.

You do know that all of the deception that surrounded you had to be revealed. A solid foundation must be laid in the beginning or the building will crack, sway and then fall. Leave all of the repair work to me. I will do what is best for you, trust my judgment. I will make it easy for you, enjoy the freedom I give. Stay open to me and I will work for you.

Laugh and be happy knowing I am working for you! Enjoy every day. Look for my hand reaching to you each single day. I will bless your efforts in rebuilding your life. How fast do you wish to travel? Just tell me the desires of your heart and I will move for you. Stay sensitive to my Spirit. Move when I say move and you will arrive at your place called "there."

You need my help. Remember that.

Abundantly,
Your Giving Father

Dear Giving Father,

Lord let it flow! I receive your abundance today. You are such an extravagant Father, giving more to me that I could ever imagine. I receive this increase that you have spoken over me and I thank you Father.

Thank you that you see my heart; keep my heart in the palm of your hand. Again today, I release those that have wounded and hurt my life. It is your hand that deals with all of us; you do keep all of the records of our lives. It is comforting to know that your heart has been touched by my pain and suffering. Because of this, I will always call upon your name.

Thank you for doing what is best for me, I cannot see everything as you see it, so my trust is in your decisions regarding the outcome of the things going on in my life.

The enemy has been uncovered; I praise you for loving me so much to do that for me. Deception and lies have no place around a believer so I rejoice for the investigation and uncovering of the enemy's plans.

Thank you for rebuilding my life. I trust your judgment, for you will give me freedom, and the way will be made smooth. Your healing has brought laughter back to my soul, thank you. I intend to enjoy every day you have given me, I watch daily for your hand reaching down into my life.

Lord you know I have always been a gas pedal, since you ask what I wanted, please move for me speedily. Even though I am a speedy believer, I want to remain sensitive to your Spirit, only moving by your direction and timing. I do need your help concerning everything…take over Lord.

In Jesus' name I pray,

Trusting fully,
Your Speedy Daughter

Psalms 13:6 I will sing to the LORD because He has been generous to me.

It Only Takes a Moment

Dear Faithful Daughter,

Do you know that it only takes a moment of time for me to react to your situation and begin to break down the walls that separate you from my miracles?

The enemy doesn't know what I intend to do for you. He can only guess, so he tries attacking from several locations hoping to stop my plan for your life. I have you safe and secure in my hand. Anything that assails you with thoughts otherwise, is a lie.

Accept where I have you now. Know that I am working out the details for your deliverance. Bloom and shine in the darkness, I still have plans for you to be used by me to bring some captives out of their prison houses.

Everything will work out for you because you are a praying woman, and I am a prayer answering Father. Moreover, I want only my hands on the steering wheel of your life. Let me take you places you never dreamed you could go. Let me immerse you in my Spirit and let me use you to flow through. If you knew everything about everything, you wouldn't need faith. Keep holding on to your faith and I will personally throw that mountain into the sea!

I am preparing you for a great end-time harvest ministry. No more will you be like Ruth in Boaz's field, picking up the leftovers; but I, your Boaz, will do what is right for you. I will bring you into my house of plenty and make you a chosen vessel fit for my purposes and plans.

You will be blessed in these latter days; my love for you will be quite evident to those surveying your life. I have filtered the happenings of your life. Remind yourself, the devil never wins, he is defeated and the greater one lives in you.

Generously,
Your Redeemer Father

Dear Redeemer Father,

Father, thank you for split-second power that has been released into my life. It has removed all hindrances to the miracles you have for me.

I thank you for the good plans you have for me. I thank you for the grace of God that enables me to prosper in you, regardless of my circumstances.

I am alert to the needs of those who cross my path, I see a need and you enable me to meet it.

Lord, you and I are a "dynamic duo" working together in your fields.

I am sitting here in the back seat, leaving all of the driving to the chief! The landscape is awesome on this journey. I am seeing places that I never knew existed.

I receive your instruction to receive a total immersion into your Spirit. Out of this experience, I give to others. I am holding to my faith and I thank you now for destroying any mountains attempting to block my way.

Thank you for doing for me what you have done for others. You are not a respecter of persons. Thank you for receiving me into your house of plenty.

I declare the enemy's demise, for my God supplies all my needs and he is my defender, my great stronghold and refuge. The greater one resides in me today and because I am his, I can face the future without fear and doubting.

Courageously,
Your faith-full Daughter

Psalms 18:2 You, LORD, are my rock and my fortress, and my deliverer; my God, my strength and in you I trust; my shield, and the strength of my salvation, and my high tower.

<u>My Warnings</u>

My Wise Daughter,

Listen carefully to my caution regarding those you should embrace. Do you know that horses can sense and smell serpents? Well, so can you! Your spirit will react when the enemy of your soul is nearby. Heed the caution in your spirit and you will escape his snare.

Rest is coming for your soul. The bruising and the stripping will stop, be mended, and healed by the Spirit of a Living God—one who sees and cares that you are hurting. Teach my truths to my people. I want them to understand that I am a Father they can truly trust with their lives.

My Word says, "Many are the afflictions of the righteous, but the Lord delivers them out of them all!" TROUBLES MAY COME, BUT TROUBLES WILL GO! Have you read, "And it came to pass?" This is the Word of the Lord to you, I keep covenant with my people and I do all that I have said that I would do.

It is time for you to pack your bags and prepare for the new journey of your life. You are getting ready to move into the world of the movers and the shakers, into the realm and dimension of the Prophets of old.

My gifts of the Holy Spirit are free, now come to my river and drink freely. Use the gifts I give to you wisely, giving all of the praise to your Heavenly Father who loves you so very much. My love reaches to the Heavens, it flows down to the lowest valley. It searches for hurting, needy people. Allow my love to flow through you, touching this world. I will use you for my praise! Begin by saying, "The Lord loves me!"

Delivering Father

Dear Delivering Father,

Thank you for your wisdom as to choosing close friends. Thank you for the caution in my spirit that the Holy Spirit gives to his children, I receive your protection today.

I receive your mending and healing of my battered emotions. You are a living Heavenly Father, one who sees my needs and responds with loving care.

As you have encouraged my heart, I will encourage others. I trust your care of me. The positive side of troubles is that they have to keep going until they pass! You have promised to deliver me from all trouble and you keep your word.

My bags are packed, point the way Father. The ministry to which you have called me has flooded my soul with excitement. I receive your wisdom to flow in the Holy Spirit with excellence.

Father I know that Jesus paid the price for me to drink from the river of life. I am drinking now, and will not stop until I thirst no more. Thank you for your love that flows to all of us regardless of how high or low our position.

I yield to your Spirit, Father. I allow you to use me to reach out to hurting mankind. I thank you that you love me just as I am.

Eagerly waiting to start,
Your wise daughter

Psalms 17:8 Keep me as the apple of Your eye and hide me under the shadow of your wings.

Sunshine

Dear Sunshine Daughter,

Set your mind on heavenly things. The enemy tried to sidetrack you, but I have intervened.

Ask me to show you the way I have marked for you to travel. You will hear, "turn this way, or turn that way." Listen carefully to me, praying always without ceasing. Talk to me all through the day and in the waking times at night. Speak to me as if I was the friend, standing right next to you. I am, you know. Tell me all that concerns you and hurts you.

Remember that after a storm, comes the sunshine. Your storm came, is passing, and sunshine beams ahead of you. Accept nothing less.

The enemy tried raining on your happiness, but his attack has missed its mark. He came to kill, steal, and destroy. Remember I am greater! I will get you the victory in this situation. Your enemy will be your footstool. Those who hurt you will have to stand before me and give an account for their deeds.

Do not ask how I am going to do this; just know that it will be done by my Spirit. I keep my promises.

Let me move more deeply in your heart and I will break up the fallow ground and plant wonderful seeds of deliverance there!

Walk the walk I have set out for you.

Bringing Deliverance,
Your Merciful Father

Dear Merciful Father,

Father my mind is set upon you. I have a made up mind.

I do desire to know the way that you want me to go. Shine your light upon the path that you have destined for me to walk. I will listen for your voice, that still, small voice that is uniquely yours.

This season of my life has been filled with violent storm activity, yet I hear you say that sunshine is just ahead. I choose to look forward to the sunshine and forget the storms. I refuse any more storm activity in Jesus' name. Thank you that the enemy's missiles missed their target. I claim total victory in this battle in Jesus' name. I know there are battles I have not even seen going on all around me, but you have protected me. In heaven some day, I will look over my life and see the whole picture, and will marvel at the battles that raged just outside my view, battles over my very life!

I thank you now for the warriors you send to help me. I know that you are a Warrior God, strong in battle. Thank you for working everything out for my good. I thank you that you keep your word.

My heart is open to you Lord. Plow up the fallow ground as needed, and plant those wonderful seeds of deliverance.

I receive this, and in the name of Jesus I pray,

Your Sunshine Daughter

Psalms 18:20 For You have caused me to run through a troop; and by You I have leaped over a wall.

Deliverance!

My Child, My Daughter,

Often you have spoken the Word of the Lord, and it manifested. Lives are forever changed when you are obedient and speak what I tell you to. These miraculous changes are not difficult for me to do through you. I now have you in a place where you know that I speak through you.

My concern now for you is that you get well. I cannot have you hurting and sad. There is much concern in Heaven and upon earth about your heartache. Remind yourself that I see things before they happen, I knew what you would need at this time of your life and I will supply it. I am not mad at you because you have not always done as much for me as you would have liked. I have seen the difficulties of your life and I will rush to make things better for you. As long as you are willing to be a vessel that I can use is all I require.

Life is not just about ministry, and what you can do for the Kingdom or me. I care about you as an individual. Others have walked away from you, but I have remained steadfast as your friend. Lay your weary head upon my shoulder and I will give you rest. I will be your friend forever.

I am sending my entire ministry staff to come and attend to your needs. Each one has been assigned a position and has a particular area of expertise to minister to you in that area. Let me help you get well, but you have to cooperate. For your part, a physician would say, "Take this pill and exercise daily." The Great Physician says, "take this faith and exercise it daily."

I know it is difficult to express your pain where you are now staying. I will make a way for you to heal and get well. I have heard your cries. Trust me that I will straighten out all of this mess. You have been faithful to reach out to others and now it is time for me to deliver you.

Bringing Deliverance,
Your Delivering Father

Dear Delivering and Healing Father,

I thank you for giving me encouragement. You know when your children need to be picked up and loved. I do know that you speak to me, that I am hearing your voice and not the voice of a stranger. I am a member of your family, and as a family member I know your voice, we have spent many years together.

Thank you that you are always looking after my well being, this knowledge makes my heart peaceful. I receive your loving touch upon the hurts of my soul, for you are the only one that can fix my problems. I thank you that you care about us as individuals, you know what we have need of even before we ask. I receive all that you have for me today.

You have been the one constant in my life, thank you for being with me through every day of my life. I now lay my head upon your shoulder for I do need a rest. Thank you for being my best friend. Thank you for the angels that have been assigned to watch over me. They have done a superb job.

Father, you know me so well! Thank you for looking after all of my needs. Thank you for hearing my cries and straightening out all of the messes. Thank you for deliverance. Oh, how I need to be delivered from the ghosts of my past, my failures, my, omissions, my sins. They sometimes try to haunt me, but I rebuke them in Jesus' name.

In Jesus' name I pray,

Your Thankful Daughter

Psalms 18:50 You have given me great deliverance and showed mercy to me, your anointed, and to my seed forevermore.

Peace and Happiness

Precious Hurting Child,

This particular time has been more painful to you because you felt at this stage in your life that you would have peace and happiness, but then suddenly you had it ripped away.

You enjoyed the laughter and I enjoyed hearing you laugh, but I was also grieved because it wasn't based on truth, but deception. That one you trusted with your life has failed and deceived you.

My heart hurts in a similar way as I see my creation with troubled mind and emotions. Would you place your hands and pray for those with troubled minds? I will anoint you to do this because you have suffered at the hands of one of them.

Your hurt will not compare to the loss felt by the one that wounded you. This person has stretched out before me, seeking relief from despair and grief. You were like a lifeline and now there is no one to hold onto. I have listened to, and responded to your petitions for this person and I have delayed judgment. Intercession can make a difference.

I will give you some understanding about the times that you are nearly overcome with sorrow about your situation. Sometimes you are discerning the one who caused your pain, feeling their sorrow, grief, and despair. Do you not understand that offenders often suffer greater grief than the offended? I can use the sorrow you feel to cause you to intercede in the Spirit so that I can move for both of you.

Prayer changes people, and prayer changes circumstances.

Patiently,
Your Omniscient Father

Dear Omniscient Father,

Thank you Father that you have already bore my grief and sorrows. Because of this, I receive healing for my broken heart. Thank you for revealing truth to me, uncovering all lies and deception from those around me.

I forgive and release anyone that has caused me pain and ask you to bless him or her. I understand by me doing this, my blessings will continue to flow, and the power of God will be released to set them free.

I will use my faith and lay my hands upon troubled minds and on the authority of your Word, you will heal them. Because you have given to me the gift of discerning of spirits, I will yield to the Holy Spirit and allow my prayers to be uttered to bring deliverance to others. I thank you that my prayers are powerful, they are backed by your power and they get results!

Father, I thank you for explaining the differing emotions that are traveling through my soul. Yes Lord, I will pray for hurting minds and emotions, I have found first hand that hurting people hurt others. I receive your anointing to pray for others' recovery.

Father, I do commit to pray for the one that wounded me so, for I cannot allow the enemy to carry that soul away.

You are right: prayer does change people and circumstances.

I am praying in Jesus' name,

Your Clear Thinking Daughter

Psalms 19:1 The heavens declare the glory of God, and the sky shows His handiwork.

Torch Light

Daughter with the torch light,

I need you to go into dark places for me. Souls need rescuing, released, and delivered! Stay humble and quiet before me and I will make my will clear and plain to you. You worry too much about making wrong turns. I can turn you and position you in the places you need to be. I'll find you if you get lost! Haven't I always?

You were already tired and exhausted before this entire last episode in your personal life. It is natural for you to fill drained and weary. You are not "superwoman", but my little woman with a torch light!"

In the Spirit, you shine brightly. In your flesh, you are weak. I can strengthen your flesh and give you many things to put back the hope, courage, and zeal that you need. Just keep receiving my grace by faith, and it shall be yours.

I am taking you back to the basics of your training. I am strengthening some things and renewing some things. Some things change, but I do not. I am steadfast and sure. And I will bring you out and bless you as you look to me as your deliverer. As you use your faith, watch me honor my Word to you.

Failure is not to be a part of anything about you. Say,"there will be <u>no</u> more failures!" Believe for success....

The enemy bombards you with thoughts of inferiority and second-class citizen syndrome thinking. You deserve more than you think. For one reason, because of what I have done for you. Second, because you have touched many lives, more than you realize. Let me bless you, get your receptors up, let me bless you...

Lovingly,
Your Steadfast Father

Dear Steadfast Father,

Father I thank you that as I humble myself today that you are making your will clear and plain to me. I thank you for your search and rescue team that finds me if I venture onto a path uncharted by your hand. I want to trust you with all of my heart knowing you have the power to keep me in your will.

Thank you for the strength you give to me any time that I have need of it. I receive your grace and the zeal and courage that only you can give. Thank you for the refresher course to strengthen some areas, and to rebuild some things that I have let slip. I thank you that you never change, I can depend upon the unwavering love that you have for me. I do look to you as the source of every need I will ever have. Thank you for honoring your Word to me, and that everything you have promised, you will deliver.

In Jesus' name, I remove the word "failure" from my vocabulary. Today is a new day filled with the promise of a bright new future. No more thoughts of inferiority and feelings of inadequacies, I am boldly approaching God's throne to obtain grace in my time of trouble. Thank you for allowing me to bless others, my receptors are up and I am listening to hear your voice. Speak Lord for your servant is listening. I open my arms Lord, and receive all that you have for me.

In Jesus' name I pray,

Undeservedly,
Your Little Woman
With A Torch Light

Psalms 20:2 Send help from the sanctuary, and strengthen me...

Strong Defender

My Needy Daughter,

I am a strong defender to those who look to me for deliverance. Sometimes my hour of deliverance comes at a time that may seem on somewhat of a time-delay schedule, but I am always on time. Little do you know, but my deliverance is happening all around you. Just keep receiving and thanking me, I will not let you down.

People pass in and out of your life. When it is time for them to pass on from your life, don't hold on; just release. Keep contact, but move forward to the new things I have for you. Determine to live for the day. Check out my miracles every day of your life.

I will begin confirming my words to you, this will help you sift the thoughts and feelings you are having. Regardless of what is going on in your life, I will still use you in the ministry. Ministry is helping people and you can certainly do that! People cross your path every day.

The "spiritual establishment" will not restrain me. I will do with you as I choose. I open doors that man cannot do a thing about!

Continue seeking my way for your life, blessings lie on that path. Flow with me. There are troubles all around, but I am your troubleshooter.

I can diagnose and repair all of your troubles and it will not cost you a penny. I operate on a level that is above normal, my level is on the supernatural level. In that realm, the gloves are removed and whatever is necessary will be done.

You often think of me on the natural level. There is nothing natural about me, everything is supernatural with me. I am more powerful than you can ever imagine. If you fully realized who I really am, and what I can do for you; it would cause your mind to blink and your heart to leap with joy. Today I say to you "try on this new piece of armor it is exactly fitted for you!"

Your Supernatural Father

Dear Supernatural Father,

I thank you that you are my strong defender, my eyes are upon you for the deliverance I need.

Thank you that your timing is always perfect. I know you are working all around me even thought I may not see it at this time. I know you will never disappoint or let me down.

I move as directed by your Spirit; I focus on this day, refusing to look into the future. Thank you for the today miracles.

Thank you for confirming your Word to me in the mouth of two or three witnesses, You have promised in your Word to do this for me. Thank you that this is protection for me, keeping me from deception and error.

I will reach out to hurting people every where I go, this is what you want me to do. Nothing or no one can stand in the way of your plans and purposes.

I flow with you! I feel your strong arms holding me. I am thankful that you are my troubleshooter.

Thank you for expense free repairs on all of my troubles. You operate on a supernatural level, and because you reside in me, so do I! Thank you for your hands on approach for my healing and deliverance.

Father I ask that you open my eyes to see all that you are. Thanks for the new fighting gear.

In Jesus' name I pray.

Thankfully,
Your Repaired Daughter

Psalms 22:4-5 Our fathers trusted in You, LORD; they trusted and You delivered them. They cried unto You, and were delivered; they trusted in You and were not disappointed!

Breakthrough

Daughter,

Get ready for your breakthrough. This is not a man-made, drummed up one, but a heaven sent Holy Ghost, power of God breakthrough.

This is the only kind that will help you. You need to see the power of a living God displayed in your life.

I will take you by the hand, lead you to a place where you can look up and see the stars. Each star represents a promise that I have made to you
.

It seems difficult right now for you to receive all I am saying to you. This is because of the intensity of the battle. Warfare is never easy and you are fighting for your life, the life that I have purchased for you.

You are in the process of crossing over, leaving the land of struggle and pain and moving into a land of lush green pastures. Indeed, the grass is greener on the other side of the fence for you!

There are some hindrances that have held you for many years and must be uprooted. They like staying in their land of familiar, but will be removed by my anointing.

My power is the greater one, and you weighing in on my side, being in agreement with my purpose and plan, has tipped the scales.

Sure victory is straight ahead.

Victoriously,
Your Powerful Father

Dear Victorious Father,

I receive my breakthrough. I thank you for allowing me to experience the power of God in my life.

Thank you for your promises. Thank you for the stars and for the promises they represent to me.

I confess, it is difficult to see past some of the smoke of battle. But, I know you have given me victory in the battles of life and I receive the spoils of war.

I am moving out of a dry barren land and into lush green pastures that are blessed by your hand. It is the Promised Land. Thank you for your mercy.

Thank you for uprooting hindrances in my life. Reveal the secret bondage's that have held me prisoner for years. Uproot them. I give you complete reign over my life. Move me as you see fit. I am packed, ready to move to a land of peace. I agree with you Lord, I am on your side. You have done great things for me, and I have the victory that was promised to me.

In Jesus' name I pray,

Your Victorious Daughter

Psalms 22:27 All the ends of the world shall remember and turn unto the Lord, and all the people of the nations shall worship before You.

The Real Truth

Dear Standing Daughter,

Do not feel condemned by your desire for restoration and the completion of my promises to you. I commend you for your fight to the finish attitude. It is easy to give up and allow your territory to be run over by bandits, but you stand and defy the odds. You will see the outcome change. Love me enough to try, and I will back you all the way.

This particular situation differs from those encountered in the past. This can be turned, believe me for a good outcome. The enemy wants to win in this, but I have placed you to stand in the gap, to pray and intercede, and cause things to turn around. Do not be afraid to hope. Stop, turn around, and face your adversary with the weapons of your warfare!

I am greater in you than the enemy that chases and barks at your life. Make him bend his knee! Use the authority I have given to you and change will come. The devil tries to make you think nothing will work against him, that all of your believing will be for nothing

.   Remember he is a liar, so rejoice that just the opposite is happening. Daughter, the words of your mouth are powerful. Stop allowing the abuse, I will back you up! There is a high level of anointing upon your lips; that is one of the reasons that I have constantly fine-tuned your heart. For out of your heart come the words that will make or break you. Give me access to your heart once more. I have healing for your heart, let me repair the damage inflicted upon your emotions.

The battles have been fierce, but I overcome all battles. I am a veteran warrior, and I am making you in my image. Fear not .The enemy is afraid of you. Nothing has worked against you. When attacked, you go to prayer and somehow he never gets done what he had planned! Congratulations on a job well done.

Proud Poppa

Dear Proud Poppa,

Father I am thankful that you understand my heart. I am happy that you do not condemn the desires of my heart to restore broken relationships. I do stand in your authority and refuse to budge one inch in believing the promises that you have made to me. In Jesus' name, I defy the circumstances standing in the way of your promises to me, In Jesus' name, I command the outcome to be as God wills.

This is a new situation and the outcome will be good for all concerned. I thank you Lord for the turning of the heart. I continue to stand in the gap, praying in faith, and the adversary must bow his knee and let go of his prisoner.

Thank you Father that you have placed within me the Holy Spirit who is greater than he that is attempting to destroy lives. I believe my prayers are highly effective, the devil is a liar, and he must take his hands off of God's property.

I refuse to allow any ground to the enemy, he was defeated at the cross by Jesus, he is stripped of his power, and I stand in the name of Jesus and I rebuke the devil.

Thank you for constantly fine-tuning my heart, I extend an open invitation to you for inspection and repair of any wounding that is located in my heart. Thank you for anointing my words, I am constantly aware of this anointing and will guard the words of my mouth. It is always my desire to bless and not curse my life or the lives of others.

You are my veteran warrior, thank you for fighting for me. I thank you that you never allow the enemy to win the fight.

Prayerfully,
Your Anointed Daughter

Psalms 23:6 Surely goodness and mercy will follow me all the days of my life and I will live in the house of God forever.

A Loving Father

Dear Daughter,

I would like to be more of a loving, nurturing Father to you. The walls you have erected keep me out and also try to keep you from interaction with those that have disappointed and wounded you in the past.

True revelation from me today would be that I say to you, "Fear not!" I want you free of fear, like a butterfly escaping from its cocoon. I see you in your struggles and I hurt to see how hard you try to break free. Enter into my rest. Allow me to heal and deliver you. Flow with me; allow my current to carry you to your destination. I love seeing the determination and the steadfastness in you. Answers will flow freely because you have persevered.

Listen to me now…. Nothing can withstand my power. Understand that deep down inside of you. This knowledge will bring you the peace and the rest that you seek.

The giant ship Titanic was said to be "unsinkable," but a bed of ice, small in comparison, caused the giant liner to sink to the ocean floor. Just as a bed of ice brought that ship down, I, with unlimited power, can deal with people great and small. You are underestimating my power to deliver you.

I have heard your prayers, the prayers of your friends, and I've seen and recognize your efforts to reach out to me. I've listened to the intercession of the Holy Spirit, and help is on the way! Stop wavering and stand strong in the Lord. Victory is in sight! Angels are returning with your goods. Your tears moved me to action and you will see the enemy put under your feet. I heard your tears, and they have caused me to respond to your needs. You will see my miracles time and time again. I have plenty to spare and an abundance to share.

As I see you bowed low before me, I will take notice and release my anointing to defend you. Ask my help in everything. Depend less on others opinions and depend more upon mine. I have much I can show you and say to you. Put on your dream cap; it shall be full of revelation!

Steadfastly,
Your Listening Father

Dear Listening Father,

According to your Word, I will enjoy the good things that you have blessed me with and I will count my blessings. Because you are helping me, I will not give up my dreams. I will not stop now or ever. I will receive all you have for me.

Thank you Father that more is going on than I can see with my eyes. You are working behind the scenes where I can't see and because of this, I am confident that you are making a way for me where there seems to be no way.

I refuse negative thoughts for you are always with me, causing good things to materialize in my life.

Father, I now realize more fully that I am in a war. There were some things I allowed the enemy to steal, but no more! I stand in Jesus' name and demand all to be returned. I command the blessings of God that has been stolen to be released to me now. Thank you for your blessings.

Thank you for giving new strength to me, so with that renewed power of God, I refuse to allow the enemy to run over me anymore. Thank you for the new determination and the new spiritual backbone. I stand up to the enemy in Jesus' name.

Father thank you that you support me 100%. Oh, so glad I am yours.

I will no longer think thoughts of defeat and lack. By your Word, I take back all that belongs to me. Thank you for those you are sending me to, I thank you for your favor that comes because of your anointing.

Steadfastly,
Your Encouraged Warrior Daughter

Psalms 23:5 The LORD prepares a table for me and my enemies can see it. HE anoints my head with oil, and his provisions for me overflow.

Giftings

Worthy Daughter,

Hear the Word of the Lord, "be a woman of faith!"

I have deposited many gifts within you, let them flow! Remain steadfast, unmovable, and you will see your Father move for you. One day you will see as I see, and understand why you were lead this way.

I want you to pray and believe that these mountains in your life will come crashing down. Listen to your heart, I will speak things to you there, and nothing shall take you by surprise.

Recognize the enemy when he speaks through others. He will use them to try to undermine your faith. Do you know that just one word from my mouth can settle all your struggles?

Seek my face, seek me and I will speak into your life.

Anger has risen against you from some of those around you. Remember that I can turn hearts in a moment of time. Trust me in this, I am working for you. I have been changing lives since man was first formed. I have the power, the wisdom, and the resources to transform lives.

Be careful that the past experiences do not shape how you will trust me. Every situation is different. I know how to turn these circumstances around for your good, for I desire the very best for your life.

Do not try figuring out how I am going to do these things. Just let me unfold them for you. It is now time for you to enter into my rest. Cease from the toil in your mind. Let me bless you without your assistance. I will straighten all the wrinkles in your circumstances and fix you in the process.

Lovingly,
Trustworthy Father

Dear Trustworthy Father,

Father, I am thankful to you for the gifting you have given me. I now open my life to you and allow them to flow to others.

I remain steadfast, unmovable to circumstances that hinders my life, and I will now see God move for me. I believe that one day soon I will have understanding about these troublesome things.

I believe I receive the promises of God, and the mountains standing in my way are crashing down. I thank you that nothing will catch me by surprise, for you tell me of things to come.

Thank you for enabling me to recognize the enemy's tactics. I only need your Word to me to settle any questions or struggling. I believe you have the power to turn a heart in a moment of time. Thank you for doing this for me.

I believe in your ability and resources to change a heart and transform lives.

I refuse to look behind me; this is a new day with new possibilities. You desire the very best for my life and I thank you for that.

I cease from attempting to determine in my mind how things will turn out, for it is your command to me to enter into your rest. I'm resting Lord....you do not need any assistance from me.

Thank you for a wrinkle free life, and the restoration of all things.

In Jesus' name I pray,

Standing steadfastly,
Your Trusting Daughter

Psalms 23:2-3 HE makes me lie down in green pastures, HE leads me beside still waters. HE restores my soul and leads me in paths of righteousness.

Don't Grieve

Daughter,

Don't grieve over the past, let me paint you a picture with a bright future, I have beautiful colors you have never seen. What has been is passed, now you must look to your future, let me make it full. I will bless you inside and out!

Every remaining day you have belongs to me. I paid to have the right to take care of you. The Good Shepherd is my name.

You have come through many devilish nightmares, this is a time in your life that I want you to rest and recover. The battles have been fierce, much has been stolen from you, but I am in the process of restoring and repairing your life. The enemy doesn't want you healed because if you recover from his attacks, and you walk healed, you then become more of a threat to his kingdom of darkness.

I will give you my peace. My peace goes beyond natural reasoning. It brings comfort to the heart when nothing else can. You must trust me now. I have your best interests at heart. We've need to work on this "trust" issue.

Many hurting souls are waiting for you to proclaim the Word of the Lord to them. Arise, you must be about the Father's business.

Continue to believe for my touch upon your life. I am speaking more details to you, listen carefully to what I am saying. I have had to challenge some of your religious thinking, and this can be a good thing. I want you to operate on a spiritual level, walking in my anointing, full of the Holy Spirit.

I now will rub your adversary's nose in the dirt. He will wish he had left you alone. He has lost again!

> Always Victorious,
> Your Loving Father

Dear Loving Father,

I thank you for healing the grieving that had tried to smother life from me. Thank you for my bright new future, I am looking with extreme anticipation to all that you have promised. It is nice to know that my time is your time, that Jesus, my Good Shepherd, owns me!

I am recovering from all the attacks of the enemy and now I am stronger than ever. The Lord strengthens me and in the name of Jesus I rebuke the hand of the enemy. Thank you for your peace, that supernatural, God-given, peace that comforts my heart.

You offer the best way in life. I am blessed beyond anything I have ever imagined. Life is good because of Jesus. Thank you for helping me, and for teaching me to trust you with all of my heart. I have jumped from my sitting position and I am giving my full attention to your call.

I believe your hand rests upon me twenty-four hours of every day, seven days a week. Thank you for maturing me, I now hear your voice and a stranger's voice I will not follow.

I have abandoned all of the religious mindsets I once held so dear, and now my mind is fixed upon Jesus and all that He says to me. Today I open my heart to the Holy Spirit and see things with eyes anointed by Him.

Thank you for rubbing the adversary's nose in the dirt. I will be eternally grateful for the great love you have for me, and the power that you have sent for my deliverance. Thank you that he has lost again and I win!

In Jesus' name I pray,

Joyfully,
Your Winner Daughter

Psalms 25:7 LORD, do not remember the sins of my youth or my transgressions. Remember me according to your tender mercies.

Your Thoughts

Dear Delivered Daughter,

Base your thoughts on what I say to you. You will never be disappointed trusting in my Word. Do not fear what others say. Bring everything to me and I will sort it all out for you. I am the only one that can. Everyone has an opinion, but you need mine!

I am doing a work in you even though you can't see me working. Naomi and Ruth couldn't see my plan in its fullness until it fully manifested. You are no different that they were. I had a plan that I worked out for their good, and I accomplished what I purposed with their lives.

Naomi didn't enjoy the loss of her husband and her only children, yet she saw abundance and replenishing in her older years. She couldn't hurry my plan; it had to unfold. I used circumstances to force her back to her roots where her blessings were.

I know where your blessings are. You must trust me and move without doubts and fears. I will sustain and keep you. I have given you those who will hold up your arms. You will make it through to victory! Face each day with hope in your heart. I would not have you hopeless. I will even provide hope. Soon this trial will be over and you will move into what I have for you. You have been my precious servant and I will reward you openly. I will not withhold your blessings out of reach but will extend my delivering hand to you in a magnificent way. You have been trying to figure things out again. This is causing the turmoil within.

Ministry will open, for I am not concerned with the past. My focus for you is the now and the forever. There are so many avenues of ministry, I can fit you in. Do not doubt me. I do love your willingness to serve me even in your own despair. I will bless your going out and your coming in. I love you, the person, and I want to help you get to a better place. You must trust me with the outcome of those things that are troubling your mind. I will give you the strength you need in these battles.

Your Heavenly Father

Dear Heavenly Father,

I choose to receive everything in life that you wish for me.

You said that if I pray according to your will that you will hear and answer my petitions.

I pray first, and I align my petitions with your will. I receive answers to every one of my prayers in Jesus' name.

I will not give up; I am holding on to my faith and trusting you with every situation in my life.

I will only speak your Word, and then I will see your miracles.

In Jesus' name, I defy the ugly circumstances in my life and the lives of my loves ones. These circumstances must change for good.

My determination to stand upon your Word is not based on a thing of the mind, but a knowing in my heart. What I see, think or feel will not move me. I will doubt my doubts and feed my faith.

Thank you for the pathway cleared and your answers arriving in style!

In Jesus' name I pray,

> Resting in Your will,
> Your Delivered Daughter

Psalms 27:11 Teach me Your way, O LORD, and lead me in a plain path.

Rest

Daughter,

You have dog paddled long enough, it's time to rest. I will give to you the rest that you seek.

Naomi and Ruth went back to Naomi's homeland to survive. The transition was rough and uncertain. They found the place where I would cause them to be blessed. Do not look at the circumstances of your life right now. Circumstances can change in the blink of an eye.

I have stretched you so far that you have felt that you would surely snap, yet I have you still in one piece.

Look for the supernatural way of provision. The higher plain is where I want you to walk. You have scratched around in the dirt long enough. Now is the time to soar with the eagles.

Fear not the rejection of man; it will not destroy your faith. I have your faith safe in my closed hand. Nothing will harm you now.

Appreciate our times together. You communicate with the Creator of the entire Universe. Do you know how many people would love this opportunity?

Blessing you daily,
The Creator Father

Dear Creator Father,

Father, I thank you for rest and peace. I thank you that you hold me in your hand and direct me to the right path. Thank you for my place of blessing, you are guiding me safely there. I don't see it yet, but my faith tells me it is beautiful. You, who created it all, own it all.

I refuse to look at my circumstances; they are changing for the good with every tick of the clock. I bless You, Father.

Thank you for the growth you are producing in my character. Nothing will move me, except you.

I'm flapping my eagle wings Lord, I may not have done so well in the beginning, but I'm getting the hang of this now. All that stretching was good for my wings. I'm sorry I grumbled so much about the training and preparation you put me through. Soaring at this height make it all worth the hard work and the struggles it took to get here.

In Jesus' name I reject rejection. I am accepted by my Heavenly Father and that is all that counts. My faith is intact, safely held in the hands of my Creator.

I thank you Father that you have allowed me to sit in your presence and to hear you speak to me. It is a great privilege and I receive this audience with you as both precious and valuable. It is healing to me, and causes me to hope in you.

Humbly,
Privileged Daughter

> **Psalm 27:5-6 For in the time of trouble, HE will hide me in his pavilion; he will hide me in the secret of his tabernacle; and he shall set my foot upon a rock. And my head will be lifted up above my enemies. I will offer sacrifices of joy and will sing praises to Him**

Speaking to You

Dear Daughter Who Dreams,

You have been hearing me speak to your heart that I have a better life for you. Forget the past and the events that have happened. Your former frame of reference is ringing in your ears and painted upon a canvas before your eyes. I will demolish the visual, and rip out the echoes in your ears.

This is a new day. It is a day of deliverance. It is a time of moving from one dimension to another. Do not fear the move, for I will hold your hand for the remainder of the journey. I will take care of you, my child. Good things are in the works.

I will set you in a place of permanence, a place of peace and rest. Others will long to come to this place for it shall even have an aroma of peace. My Word says, "though the vision tarries, wait for it." This scripture demonstrates your life now. Many things that I have promised to you are ready to materialize. I am making you into a woman of peace, one that doesn't hurry or worry. This is a great work I am doing in you. Listen for my voice, I will speak to you. Sometimes I will speak directly to you, other times it will be through another. You will see my hand at work in you. The truth of my Word to you will be evident.

Why are you afraid to try? You do not need anyone's permission to pursue hard after me. Daughter, dream big dreams for me. Many of your dream failures in the past were because of those who were surrounding you. They pulled you back as you dared to dream.

I placed the dreams of your heart there. Even though they didn't fully manifest back then, they are still alive and well within your heart. I knew when I placed my dreams within your heart just how long it would be before they became a reality. Try again, and guaranteed success will be yours.

Blessings,
Your Dream Giver Father

Dear Dream-Giver Father,

You are an awesome Father. First of all, I want to thank you for speaking to me. Thank you for this new day of deliverance from the past failures and hurts of yesterday. Thank you for this work of grace to me

I have needed the past photo gallery in my mind of the things gone sour to be removed. Thank you for removing the recordings being played in my ears, words of failure and defeat.

I believe I am moving from one dimension to another and I will not fear the move. Why should I fear, for you have my hand in yours. Your care of me is wonderful to see, and I thank you for the good things you are giving to me.

Thank you for this place of permanence, no more tent dwelling for me. I thank you for this place of peace and rest.

I am thankful for this work of peace that is being accomplished by your hand. I need peace to live in this troubled world. I will not hurry or worry.

I thank you for this season when all of those things you have promised are materializing. I hear your voice as you speak with me.

Here goes Lord, I will attempt those big things that are being placed in my heart to do for you. I am trusting that you will give success to my efforts. My dreams are back in place, I move forward with anticipation of their fulfillment.

You are the dream giver, and the dream maker.

I thank you in Jesus' name,

Expectantly,
Your Dream-Believing Daughter

> **Psalms 27:1 The LORD is my light and my salvation. Who is there to fear? The LORD is the strength of my life. Who is there to be afraid of?**

Dare To Dream

Dear Visionary Daughter,

Try again, dare to dream again. I hold the clock and the calendar in my hands. I have marked the days and I know when the dreams will become reality. Let me tell you again, I am the dream giver and the dream fulfiller.

Many around you think you are "down for the count," but the champion who lives within you will breathe new life and vitality into your being. Your bruised and wounded heart will be healed and I will give you something to laugh about.

I will place road markers all along the road where I want you to walk. Do not fear the future. Relax, sit back and watch your Lord fight for you. The best truly is yet to come. I tenderly watch over every detail of your life.

The key to a better life is listening carefully to what I have to say and obeying the instructions fully. Guaranteed results will follow! You have heard the saying, "the best laid plans of mice and men often go astray." You need my plans and blueprints to build anything successful for me.

I would have my people come and truly worship me. I visit in the praises of my people. I have my plans and I will not let man control and dominate, running everything. I will not fight man in this arena, I will simply remove myself from the endeavor. What is left will be without signs and wonders.

You are a visionary, run with my vision. I will help you fulfill my purposes for your life. When those around you laugh and mock, they are doing the same to me. They are saying that I am unable to keep the promises I have made to you. The one laughing last will be you. It will be laughter of completeness given to you by your Heavenly Father.

Well done, my daughter. Today you have made points with me!

Pleased Father

Dear Pleased Father,

I thank you for all of my dreams coming true. You are the dream giver and the dream maker. Thank you for restoring my dreams, and along with it, hope.

Thank you that when others see me as down and out, you see me as moldable clay, becoming a vessel of your choosing. The breaking of my old vessel has made me bruised and wounded. Thank you that you can make me better than new. Master, mold me with the dreams you have for my life.

My champion who lives within me has put me back on my feet, and I am ready to continue the race. Thank you for laughter and healing for my soul.

Thank you for the clearly marked path that you have for me. I will not fear where it leads because you always have my best interests at heart.

My ears are open to hear the Word of the Lord, I only want to walk in your pathways. Father help me to yield to the leading of the Holy Spirit. I want to see your signs and wonders.

I will run with the vision you have placed within me, and you will fulfill all of the promises you have made to me. You are more than able, to do those things you have said you can do. Faithful is your name.

I love laughter, especially when I see my dreams coming true.

Waiting eagerly,
Your Dream Believing Daughter

> **Genesis 37:5—Joseph had a dream, and when he told it to his brothers. They hated him all the more. (From Dreams to Destiny was 13 years)**

Unlikely

Dear Likely Daughter,

You know from your own life I can raise up unlikely workers in my fields of harvest

Paul was unlikely. Rahab, the harlot, was unlikely. Ruth was unlikely. Moses was unlikely. Mary Magdalene was unlikely. Even the babe born in a stable was unlikely.

Why do you question my ability to work with you and through you? Do you not think that I can raise up workers from broken clay? I breathed into the first clay; I can breathe into you as well. You are my creation. I have seen everything, and I, the God who created the universe, desire to use you as my vessel. I have a work only you are suited for. Trust me! I am God. I am pleased with your willingness. You are worthy because I am your righteousness. It is your inheritance.

Study this with me. How many have you read about that was perfect. Yet, they allowed me to perfect them for the work I had for their lives. There isn't a lot of time to waste; so my Spirit will do a quick work with you. There are souls to rescue and to save. I need an agent with your exact qualifications, understand this.

First, let me deal with a hindrance. I want you to trust me with your finances. You are set free from the spirit that causes poverty, lack, and want. Finances will go from a trickle to a flood, over the banks and onto surrounding grounds.

Poverty's power is broken for sure. Speak with authority. I have given you this authority. Enforce it. Mix faith with this word because it is my desire to move you from lack to plenty.

Keep a record of my faithfulness to you. I am going to give you more than enough. Let the record begin today.

Powerfully,
Your Righteous Father

Dear Righteous Father,

Father, I thank you for looking in the heart of man and not on outside appearances. My outside appearance, at times, has been pretty shabby looking. I have often looked like a failure. I am humbled that you would even look at me to be a child of yours.

You make me likely. My righteousness is nonexistent except that my righteousness is from you. Use me Lord. I know the establishment might look at me and stamp me "rejected." You stamp me "beloved." -- Lord, I love you. I might love you a little more than some, because I have so much to be thankful for. My mind is made up. I am yours, forever, for whatever.

It would make me very happy to have you use me for your purposes.

Thank you for the quick work you are doing in my life.

I trust you for my finances for your name is "Faithful". Because poverty is under the curse and Jesus has bought me back from that curse, I have every right to be blessed by you.

I receive all that you have for me today. I am content with my present finances. I agree with you, Lord, for everything you desire to give me as a blessing. Thank you.

You have said that you want my finances to go from a little, to abundance, so I believe for your desires to come to me in Jesus' name.

I'm excited to see what you are doing in my life, my Father. Thank you for taking time to speak to me today.

In Jesus' name I pray,

Humbly,
Your Blessed Daughter

> **Psalms 30:11 You, LORD, have turned my mourning into dancing; You have taken off my garments of mourning and dressed me with gladness.**

Don't Give Up!

Dear Delightful Daughter,

Do not give up until you have everything I have promised. I feed you the bread of life. I am the one who stands you upon a stool so you can be seen. You remain sweet, and I will do it all for you. Trust in me even when you can't see it working out. Trust in my power to protect and keep you safe.

I want to use you for my praise. Man would keep the doors shut, but I will make my own door that will open. People will be amazed as I sit you in your place called there. I do have that place for you. Do not worry about those who will stand by your side, I will put around you a wall of fire. My angels will get the job done.

Now that the enemy has stripped you of the things you counted upon, this is when I can show you my power and my glory. I delight in making your dreams come true.

You are bringing everything and laying it all at my feet. What a delightful daughter you are. Because your situation looked so hopeless you have become fearful. Your enemy has rehearsed his plan for your life, but you should have rejoiced. You must remember that he is a liar and he tells the opposite of what is truth.

I will always be right beside you in everything you have to walk through. This knowledge should help. Yes, you have some major things going on in your life, but nothing that baffles me. I know exactly what must be done to deliver you. Now you are more wary, and this will be beneficial for you.

I haven't forgotten you. You are receiving lessons in faith. Nothing can stop you now. We're both on the same side and I will add my faith to your faith and you will see a mountain-moving explosion of my Spirit. Do not be so intense, you don't have to beg or force me to move for you. I back you 100%.

Powerfully,
Your Omniscient Father

Dear Omniscient Father,

I will not give up! I receive everything that you have promised to me. Thank you for your power that protects and keeps me. Thank you for my place called there. I walk through the door you have opened.

Your angels are standing by my side. They are a wall of fire all around me. I thank you that they complete every task they are given. Father I thank you that you are adding back to me the things that have been stolen, thank you for being a restorer of shattered dreams.

I no longer listen to the story the enemy has tried rehearsing in my mind, I submitted myself to you, I resisted him and he has fled in terror! I receive your truth and bind his lies in Jesus' name.

Thank you for your plan for my deliverance. I thank you that nothing about my situation worries you. I receive your wisdom to make wise decisions, not letting my unwise mercy cloud the wisdom and discernment that you give to me.

Thank you for these lessons in faith, now I can say, "I will not be stopped in Jesus' name!"I thank you that we are on the same team and because of this, I receive the experience of a mountain-moving explosion of the Holy Spirit.

Thank you for your 100% guaranteed backing. I walk in your great adventure for my life. I am so glad that you give freely and that I do not have to beg or try to force you to move. Again, thank you for additional advice and counsel.

Contentedly,
Your Relaxed Daughter,

Psalms 23:4 Even though I walk through the valley of the shadow of death, I will fear no evil for you are with me and your strength comforts me.

Money Containers

Dear Wise Daughter,

I want to speak to you again about your finances. Learn to trust me where your needs are concerned. I own everything and everything is at my disposal.

I can present miracles at any given moment of time, and I work best when I work in the lives of my children. I move resources around.

You cannot understand my timing or my reasons. It would be like explaining chemistry to a nursing infant. I am sorry daughter, but it is over your head. The simple thing for you is to believe, trust, and exercise your faith.

Exercising your faith means you must determine in your heart to believe what I have promised. Make a decision to believe. If you believed effortlessly, it would not take faith. Take a faith walk and build up those faith muscles.

I will refill your money containers. This is not difficult for me to do. Believe. I will show you what to do. I have always provided for you. This time keep it intact, keeping prying fingers out of the bag. I have given you wisdom and a merciful heart, balance the two.

Hearing by my Spirit is precious and valuable. My beloved children move when I say move. Many love hearing from me and allow my Spirit to send blessings through them. A portion of these blessings is reserved for you. Can you believe?

I want you to live a life of faith. Great men and women of God in times past tested and tried me. They found nothing lacking in me. And I change not....I am the same for you. I will bring the ministry to you, not you to it. I will open that door. I will speak clearly leaving no doubt as to what you are to do.

Generously,
Your Wealthy Father

Dear Wealthy Father,

I thank you for blessing me again, for restoring my finances. I will surely try to balance wisdom and mercy. I receive your advice regarding how to handle your blessings. I will keep prying fingers out of the money you give to me. Wisdom will be my word for each day. I am truly appreciative for all of the income you send my way.

I realize I cannot understand or know all that you are doing in my life. Thank you for allowing me a peek into what is happening. Even then, your ways must be explained to me by your Spirit. Your economy and your bookkeeping are far too complex for a mere mortal. Human financial systems are all bottom line, full of greed and selfishness, but yours is filled with mercy and grace.

I want to operate in godly economics. I will give and have it multiplied back to me, but I will use wisdom in my giving. I will listen to your Spirit.

I thank you that you will fill my money containers. You have always provided for me. I realize when I look at my empty money containers; I panic, because I have trusted in them, and not you.

You are the same faithful God of men and women that have gone before me; their faith was rewarded every time, and so will mine. I will lack nothing for you have said that you would not withhold any good thing from me.

Thank you that you treat all of your children alike, there are no favorites with you.

I receive your clear instructions as to what to do with the life and resources that you have placed in my hands.

In Jesus' name I pray,

Humbly,
Your Wise Daughter

> **Psalms 31:19 Oh, how great is Your goodness, which You have laid up for your own servants...**

Final Push

Dear Expectant Daughter,

You are feeling that final push like a woman feels as the baby emerges. Push and rest, the end is in sight. I will change your focus. I can do anything I like with your life; this is because you have handed it over to me.

Things take some time to change. Hurts go away gradually; some of the things that have happened in your life have driven you to me. I am the only one that can help you.

Mix your faith with patience. All of these things you already know, but what I am teaching you now is about my faithfulness to you during this period of your life. I would like for you to remember that I will not forget what you have done for my kingdom.

Now I would like for you to mobilize prayer teams, have prayer retreats and encouragement sessions. Agreement between believers produces great results. Keep praying and this will cause a continual flow of answers to come your way. At times, try adding some fasting, and expect answers!

Continue to make it your aim to mind your own business. Keep away from judging my servants. I am the judge.

Trust what you hear from me, for I do speak to you. You are hearing more than you think, your mind is often afraid to acknowledge it. Keep your ear tuned to me and revelation about many things will be given.

A celebration is in store for you. A warm welcome with a welcome mat engraved with your name is being rolled out for you. It will be a joyful time.

Preparing the Way,
Patient Father

Dear Patient Father,

I thank you that the end of this battle is in sight. I receive your help to focus on positive things and not on the negative circumstances staring me in the face.

Thank you for the faith of the Lord that is within me, and now I enter into trust and patience to see you bring me into a spacious place, safe from the reach of my enemies.

Your memory is truly awesome, never forgetting a thing. You have seen the things I have done for your kingdom, and you will reward me openly. Thank you that your mercy keeps you from remembering my sins; yet instead you see me as righteous.

This is difficult for my heart to understand because others point out my failures. I am one who has so much to be thankful for. I love you Father.

I will obey you and have the prayer gatherings, and see the results of the power of agreement when believers come together and agree upon your Word.

It is my desire to mind my own business, I am not in any position to poke my nose in the lives of others, and I will keep myself occupied with the issues that I have to deal with.
You will take care of the things needing attention, for you are the judge of all the earth.

Thank you for speaking to my heart and mind; I am so privileged to be in your family. I receive all that you wish to say to me. Thank you for the celebration that you have planned for me, I know it will be first class all the way!

In Jesus' name I pray,

> Obediently,
> Your Hearing Daughter

Psalms 31:16 Make your face shine upon me, Lord.

Not Down

Dear Still-Standing Daughter,

Many around you think that you are down for the count. Friends and family have turned, though a few remain. Have you noticed I have sent you encouragement along the way?

The champion who lives within you will now breathe in new life and vitality. Your bruised and wounded heart will be healed and I will give you something to laugh about.

If I had allowed this last situation to be turned, there would not have been this preparation time for you to do something gigantic for me. Remember that all things work to my advantage for those who love me and fulfill my purposes. You are one of those. All things include this thing you are going through.

Now you have mounted the horse, your feet are in the stirrups and you are ready to run the race. Right now, do not concern yourself with other situations. I will take care of everything.

I will place road markers all along the road that I want you to take. Do not fear the future, relax, sit back and watch your Lord fight for you. The best truly is yet to come for you.

Just as I tenderly took care of you before, I will watch tenderly over every detail of your life. The key to a better life is listening carefully to what I have to say and obeying the instructions fully. Guaranteed results will follow. I am pleased with your progress.

Tenderly,
Your Tender Father

Dear Tender Father,

Thank you for lifting me up from the mat where the enemy of my soul had me slammed. I felt like slinking under a rock. I am thankful that the greater one, my champion Jesus, is still alive and doing the things today as he did when he walked the shores of Galilee. You have not changed. You are the same to me today as you were to those of yesterday. You are alive and well upon planet earth.

Thank you for your healing of my emotions, and for the newness that you have imparted. Thank you for the promise of laughter, your Word says that laughter does me good like medicine. I take my dose today, and feel so much better. Thank you for the encouragement and for the those you send who encourage me.

Thank you for this time alone with you, I am on the right road and have heard your Word for me to run the race. Thank you for the well-marked highway that leads to my destination. I will enjoy the trip. I can ponder and appreciate the better life that is in your hand. You have proved that you attend to all of my needs and I sincerely appreciate how carefully you watch over my life. I will listen to your instructions and obey them.

I want your plans, not mine. Pull back the curtain and let me look in. Lord, please help me to do all things according to your instructions. Please stay on the premises, for I love signs and wonders. I hear you say that I am a visionary; imprint your vision before my eyes. Regardless of what others think; I shall have everything that you have promised, because you keep your word.

Thank you for being pleased with my progress.

With joy,
Your Laughing Daughter

> **Psalm 32:11 Be glad in the LORD, and rejoice, all you righteous; and shout for joy, all you who are upright in heart.**

What Does It Profit?

Dear Profitable Daughter,

What does it profit if you gain the whole world and lose your soul? If you work for me, you will gain both in this world and the world to come. Release yourself to me and I will work wonders for you. Your employer will be the "The God of the whole earth!" I have an excellent benefit package, frequent promotions, and an adjustable pay scale. I can take you farther than you ever expected to go, this is providing that you apply yourself. You are not ordinary. I have made you to be extra ordinary. Stop trying to be ordinary.

Let anxiety fall by the wayside, I have you firmly in my grip, you will not fall. You can never accomplish the things you need to do staying in your present circumstance. Your arms will be held up instead of hanging down. I will add many children and grandchildren to you. Your remaining years will be filled with promise. Continue to stand and believe me for the return of that which has been stolen. I want you blessed. I will do a quick work, no more wasted years.

Trust in me, I have not forgotten you. Keep in mind the importance of obeying my voice. Do not listen to others. Wear the ministry-mantle that I have given specifically to you. It contains precious treasures, meant to bless the world. I will move you swiftly into it. I will surround you with my protection, fear not nor shrink back. I will be with you.

Stay where I put you until I tell you to move. Sometimes you are to stand still because of timing, other times it will be because I simply say "no!" Father knows best.

Now that you are back on track, we are ready to move forward. Trust me with all of your heart and lean not to your own understanding. I have need of you in my fields. Give hope and encouragement to those people that I send you to. Many rewards for faithful service are awaiting you for the things you have done for others.

Well Pleased,
Father of Faithfulness

Dear Father of Faithfulness,

I thank you for the day you introduced yourself to me. I didn't know how much I needed your love; yet you came to me anyway. Given my history, what would I have done without you? No treasure could compare to you. I release myself, again, today to you.

Eternity lasts forever but this world with all of its glitter will pass away like a vapor. I love belonging to you, and I will discipline myself to complete the things that you have placed in my hands to do. Thank you for the extra ordinary life that I live.

Living in your hands is the best security I could ever hope for .Your wisdom knows what I need and where I can find it.

Thank you for placing people in my life that will help me fulfill all that you have desired me to do. I receive your promise of a blessed life. I believe for everything that has disappeared from my life to be returned promptly. The promise of no more wasted years, and the quick new thing that you are doing in me, refreshes my soul and encourages my heart.

You keep perfect books. You provide double recompense for my troubles. You know me inside out. Your judgment is fair. I trust in your mercy and love. You surround me with your protection so I will not fear anything.

I will remain stationary until I hear you tell me what to do and where to go. Thank you for the anointing of the Holy Spirit, I am blessed that you would anoint me to minister the gospel of Jesus Christ. I enter the fields of harvest with you Lord; I am ready to work for you. I will share your hope and encouragement to hurting people everywhere. Thank you for all you have done for me.

In Jesus' name I pray,

Safely,
Your Faithful Employee

Psalms 34:11 Come, children, listen to me. I will teach you the fear of the LORD.

People Pressure

Daughter,

Because your ears need to hear it again, I will tell you again. You are not ordinary. I have a special plan for your life that the ordinary person could not do. Do not let people pressure you into doing what they think is good for you. Do what feels comfortable to you.

Move at a pace where you have peace within. Your spirit will react when things are out of order.

Listen to your inner voice, He, the Holy Spirit, guides with such precision, no mistakes or miscalculations. Move by my Spirit, he will get you safely to the place I have called you to.

Tell your mind "be still, and take a seat in the corner," and then you watch the ways of the Lord. I can do more for you in one moment than you can do in a lifetime.

Forget the past, yesterday is gone with all of its victories and its sorrows. You have the present and the future. I intend to fill it with good things. Take a deep breath and let the worries of your life slip away. Don't worry about anything; I have everything under my control.

Just as the early church was scattered because of persecution and the word about Jesus was spread wherever they went, I have some people who sit in darkness that need the Word of Life. I am sending you to them.

Your Commander Father

Dear Commander Father,

Father I place my feet in the footprints of your steps. The pressure of others does not move me, and my peace remains intact.

I am confident that the Holy Spirit alerts me if my steps need correction. His assistance keeps my feet in step with the beat of his heart.

I listen to the Holy Spirit's voice, receiving his precise instructions to the place where I belong. My mind is seated, out of the way, and I am watching my Father perform his miracles.

I am walking in the good things of God, the past is gone forever, and the Spirit of the living God has erased it from my mind.

The Lord has everything in my life under his control so I do not have to worry. The worries of my mind leave in his presence.

Lord I choose to be flexible and pliable in your hands. I will be obedient to share those precious things that you speak to my heart.

Sometimes Father, because I have been so burdened, and I have been through so many trials, that I often forget that everything isn't just about me. This causes me to temporarily forget my calling, that high calling, to carry light into dark places. I rest my mind now, I now choose to think about what you have for me to do for you. I pick up my torch, now, Lord. I will keep my lamp trimmed and burning, ready to go. I hear the command, "The Lord has need of you."

> Patiently,
> Your Obedient Daughter

> **Psalms 34:17 The righteous cry, and the LORD hears and delivers them out of all their troubles.**

I Love You

To My Prayerful Daughter,

I love you so much that I will never give you something that will hurt you.

Listen carefully, I love you so much that I will not give you something that will hurt you.

Unanswered prayers in one area are actually answered prayers. I always hear. You are my beloved. I know what is best.

I simply said, "no."

Now it is time for you to be prospered. I want you content with the provisions I have given to you, but now I want you to also stretch your faith to receive all that I now have for you.

I am capable of giving more than trickles of blessings. I am the God of overflow.

Look with expectancy for unexpected miracles. I am King over the entire earth. I own everything.

Prayer-Answering Father

Dear Prayer-Answering Father,

It is so nice to have someone who truly loves me. Your love was demonstrated to all people that you gave the very best you had. You loved us when we were so unlovely.

Your son, Jesus, came to this diseased and dying planet to offer a way to have a new life, one where we will live eternally with you; that is incredible love. You loved me while I was so unlovable. Thank you.

I am thankful for all the provisions you have already blessed me with, and now you have spoken that you want to enrich my life again.

I receive all that you desire to give to me. I have stretched my faith, and I am watching and expecting these good things to come to me.

Your Word of overflow captivates me. This sounds so good to me, I receive the overflow blessings now.

I look to you now with expectancy; I know miracles are coming my way.

Everything belongs to you.

In Jesus' name I pray,

The King's Prayerful Daughter

> Psalms 34:18 The LORD is near those who are of a broken heart, and saves those with repentant spirit.

Let Me In

Daughter,

Let me into your life. My desire is to care for you better than you can ever imagine.

I am taking more control of your life now. Relax and rest, the battles have been fierce, now you must rest and get well.

I have brought you to this place to care for you. Others try to help, but I know what you need.

Do not battle in your mind regarding these personal situations, I need to have full authority here, I will handle the entire affair.

There is nothing in your own strength that you can do. The part you have in this is to pray, speak the Word, and believe me.

Others will disappoint and let you down. Know that I am here to guide and keep you. Forgive, bless, and move on.

When those that have hurt you see how I have caused you to be blessed, their attitudes will change.

I see hearts, and I am telling you now that the one that caused you such heartache is in the midst of crisis and turmoil. Things are not going as smoothly as was expected. I know all things.

Lovingly,
In-Charge Father

Dear In-Charge Father,

Father I place my life into your hands. Because of your great love and power, I will do this without reservation

.

Today I receive your healing touch upon my life. Even though I have had some fierce encounters, you now give me rest and relaxation.

I am so glad that I have been blessed, and you allow me to observe the ways you are providing for me. You have done more than my little brain could even imagine.

I have now placed my personal situations in your hands, so I am not going to concern myself with one bit of it, you are the authority here.

Your strength is what I depend upon, I will pray, believe, and speak the Word and you will do the rest.

Thank you for your guidance, and for your keeping power. I release everyone that has done evil to me, and I ask you to bless them. My hope is in you Lord, for you are consistently faithful.

Everyone that looks upon me will see how marvelously you have cared for my life. Touch hurting hearts this day.

I pray in Jesus' name,

Watchfully,
Your Blessed Daughter

Psalms 36:7 How excellent is thy loving-kindness, O God! Therefore, the children of men put their trust under the shadow of thy wings.

On Assignment

Daughter,

All that has happened is not entirely about you, but is about my eternal purposes.

I will use you to reach into dark places, using the torch that I have placed in your hand, and you will light fires for the Kingdom of God.

There are many traps along the way, so walk carefully. Hear my voice, obey me, and I will keep you safe from all harm.

Let my living water flow over your emotions. It will bring healing everywhere it goes.

My power is limitless; there is enough for the entire world to experience.

In My hands,
Father

Dear Father,

I accept the assignment you have for me. Your will is my first purpose.

Help me to look beyond what is happening around me and see the whole picture. I realize now that the enemy has tried to set a trap for me.

Thank you for the torch that has been placed in my hand. I will use it to light dark places and light fires for all to gather around and be warmed by your presence.

Father please hold my hand and guide me safely around the enemy's traps. You know where safe ground is, so show me where to step.

Father, place me under your faucet and run your living water over my soul. Thank you for it's healing power... I receive it now.

In Jesus' name I pray,

Patiently,
Your Torch Light

> **Psalms 36:9 For with You, God, is the fountain of life; in Your light we will see light.**

You Sought Me

Dear Seeking Daughter,

You sought me today, and I have responded with help for your needs. I have handpicked gifts that are coming into your life. These gifts are for your needs in this life, and in the supernatural realm also. I have new Gifts of the Holy Spirit for you to use to bless others.

Prepare your heart for this new gifting for it is an awesome mantle, carried by great saints of old. Once operational, everyone will know you have been with me.

Life, as you know it, is getting ready to change. This new dimension will bring change in many areas of your life. You will go from "just enough," to "abundance enough to share." I will replace shame with honor, and sickness to health. There will be more of me in you.

It is time for these promises to materialize. I will prove to you that I keep my promises. Your mind is not always so sure about that. The things that I have purposed to give to you will be greater than your mind has dared to hope for. In all of this time of waiting, the only thing I required was for you to believe that one-day I would manifest this to you.

When your promises arrive, you will see my great love. I wish to bless you for you have blessed my heart as you have reached out to help others even while your own struggles were very great. No matter what you think others might think of you, remember what I think of you.

Let me take you by the hand and show this new gift to you. I believe you will be happy with my choice for you. When you share the news of my blessings upon your life, the receiving of promises, teach my people that I give because of promises made many years ago to Abraham, and tell them that they are of his seed.

Lovingly,
Promise Keeping Father

Dear Promise Keeping Father,

Thank you, Father, for responding to the cries of my heart. What a thrill to be an heir of God, to receive the blessings given to Abraham.

I receive all of the Gifts the Holy Spirit has for me. Thank you for the grace to walk in this new mantle that is being placed upon my shoulders. I stay in your presence, desiring to please you in all of my ways.

Thank you for change, for the shift into more of you and less of me. Everything I am or ever hope to be, it is all because of your hand upon me.

Thank you for the promised abundance, and for the removing of the old and the gift of the new.

Forgive the times my mind tried to doubt the integrity of your Word. I want to walk at all times in the faith of God.

I thank you Father that you know me from the inside out. I am touched when I hear you say that you are pleased with me.

Father I am dressed and ready to go. Lead the way.

Waiting and watching,
Your Daughter of Abraham

Psalms 37:11 But the meek shall inherit the earth, and shall delight themselves in the abundance of peace.

Look to Me

Dear Prayerful Daughter,

Just look to me in prayer, and I will answer those prayers. Use the faith I have given you and a way will be made for you. Let me care for your problems, throw yourself into my capable arms, they will carry you.

I have hidden you away with me and great fruit will come because of this alone time with me.

I am working in your behalf. Cease from striving, and enter into my rest. I have rest and peace for you that you have yet to experience. Trust me in everything and the peace will come.

I have used you in the place you are currently residing. I have caused dead and dying embers to be stirred, and I have brought hope to those who felt all hope was gone.

You have entered into a place where I will support you to the fullest. My power is at your disposal, use it wisely. A great price was paid for its availability. I am standing beside you now feel my presence.

My son poured out his lifeblood so that new life could be given to hurting mankind, go tell others of my great love for mankind.

Protectively,
Your Advocate Father

Dear Advocate Father,

I have talked to you about all of the things surrounding my life, and now I thank you for fixing every one of them.

I am running into your loving arms for they are strong and mighty, I will stay close to your side until my journey is completed.

How marvelous to spend quiet private time with you, the improvements in me are amazing. Thank you for the increase of peace and rest. My trust is in your unfailing love.

Your hand upon me has caused others to be renewed, refined, and set ablaze by your Spirit. Because of the alone time spent with you, I have understanding of your ways. It is interesting to watch you bring people into my life, and how I am now sharing these insights with others.

I receive with humility and carefully walk in the precious anointing of the Lord, never forgetting the price that was paid for its availability.

Thank you, Jesus, for paying the price with your life. It is because of your giving to us, that now, hurting people can approach your throne and receive help in their time of trouble.

In Jesus' name I pray,

Still marveling at your mercy,
Your Trusting Daughter

Psalms 37:24 Though I fall, I will not be utterly cast down; for the LORD upholds me with HIS hand.

Live Each Day

Beloved Daughter,

Live each day to the fullest. Allow my presence to saturate your entire being. I do have a healing and restoration for the mind and emotions.

The enemy has placed extreme displeasure in the hearts of some people close to you. His desire for you was to keep you under his thumb, wanting the remainder of your life to stay in the place of defeat, failure, and shame. It was that spirit that wanted to cast upon you a feeling of embarrassment. I have not allowed the plan of the enemy to prosper, I have brought you out.

Ahead is a bridge for you to cross, you will go from one place to another.

This is occurring in the spirit and in the natural. Once across, you will experience a life beyond anything you could have ever imagined. Do not look back to what might have been. I have told you, "I have greener pastures for you!" Trust me that I will give to you a better way of life.

I can move you if I choose. Do not forget that I have great power and abilities. When I placed you upon the earth, I purposed to lovingly care for you. My hand has brought you through many troubled places, now that I have your full attention, I can do all that I have promised that I would do.

Do everything that I have placed in your heart; be diligent with what I place before you. People will be amazed at the work of my hands. Faith is having absolute trust in me.

The way that you have been forced to walk recently has been hard for you. Your body has responded to the pressures of these experiences, but as you settle again, restoration will be experienced.

Walk away from anything that troubles you. I want to restore your peace and trust. I will show myself faithful to you.

Lovingly,
From Father

Dear Father,

Father, your presence saturates my being. Thank you, Lord, for healing and restoration in my life. It is my determined decision that each day will be lived with gusto.

For those who have yielded themselves to the adversary and caused me sorrow, I ask that you forgive them. They were unaware of the pressure being placed upon my soul.

My life of failure, defeat, and shame is over and done with. Father, you have delivered me from embarrassment and rubbed the enemy's nose in the dirt. Thank you for the bridge ahead of me. I enjoy new experiences and I look with expectation to a new life filled with your promises.

I refuse to look back to what might have been. I desire your greener pastures. Thank you for your great power and abilities. I am glad you chose me. I am glad I answered "yes" when you called.

My full attention is upon you Lord and I thank you for your loving care. Open my eyes and ears to know what it is that you require of me. My skeptics will be amazed that you want to use me. My faith is steady and rock solid, and by your grace it will remain that way until I stand before you.

You have proved to me that you are a faithful Father, thank you for relieving the pressures and stress of my life. I am taking your advice and staying out of situations that cause my peace to disappear.

In Jesus' name I pray,

Trusting,
Your Peaceful Daughter

Psalms 37:40 And the LORD will help me and deliver me. HE will deliver me from the wicked and save me because I trust in HIM.

Keep Seeking Me

Daughter,

Keep your heart and mind seeking me, and I will give you rest.

There is a limitless supply of my power and it is available to my children. Feast upon my bounty and expect supernatural deliverance. I continually operate on the level of the supernatural. I love confounding the wise.

Nothing will stop you now, I have issued the orders for your breakthrough and it will be sweet! As you pray and sit in my presence I will reveal myself to you.

One of the things that holds back your hope is an inability to believe that finally after all that you've been through, that I can still do all I have promised. Do I not do all things well?

Do I know what you need? Of course I do, I will give you the desires of your heart.

I desire a full life for you. Do not be afraid to hope that I will supply all that you desire. I love giving good things to my children.

Let down your hair and begin to laugh and have fun again. I will give you one to share this laughter with.

Joyfully,
From Father

Dear Joyful Father,

I am at rest now because my heart and mind are upon you.

I am so fortunate to have a limitless Father, one who is supernatural. Father, all of your children are blessed to call you daddy.

Thank you for the wisdom you impart to me. Unbelievers are amazed at the way you work.

It is good to know that "orders from headquarters" have already been issued, and I taste the sweetness of your provisions. Your presence floods my soul as I sit in your presence.

Lord I now realize that regardless of the lateness of the hour, you can, and you will, do all that you have promised.

Everything you do is excellent. Thank you for giving to me the desires of my heart. You have a wonderful heart toward your children. We bask in your love.

Joy is returning to my life, I thank you for the release of laughter and fun.

This laughter has relaxed my hairstyle and now I am as free as a breeze.

In Jesus' name I thank you,

Joyfully,
Your Bountiful Daughter

Psalms 39:40-41   I waited patiently for the LORD, and he inclined unto me, and heard my cry. He brought me out of a horrible pit and set my feet on a rock, and established my goings. He put a new song in my mouth.

Excessive Pushing

Dear Daughter,

Anything that requires excessive pushing and pressure is not of me. When I show you a direction to take and hindrances appear, step back and allow me to prepare the way.

Things I want accomplished will be completed by my power and might. There is much left to be done, so let me show you how you can best be used by me.

I am not in a panic that the world is spinning out of control, I control the entire universe, and it spins by my Word. Be a strong woman of faith. I have showed to you my faithfulness and I will continue to do so, and my great favor will rest upon you.

The one that has injured your heart mocked me as his evil plans of deception were set in motion. Now I am involved in resolving these issues. Mocking his creator and my chosen vessel will bring more trouble to the mocker than he has ever had in his lifetime.

The mocker has also injured others, and you too were touched by his evil. Remember I can be a God of love and mercy and a God of divine judgment. This deception cannot be overlooked. This is out of your hands now. I decree certain things and until my appointed time period is concluded, nothing can change my dealings.

For every day you were lied to, every day you suffered devastation, and for every day spent in physical and financial stress, for all of this, full payment will be required. All involved will have my dealings in their lives. People must realize there is a reaping for bad seeds sown.

Let me handle all of this.

Protectively,
Your Father

Dear Protective Father,

I thank you that I have entered into your rest. I refuse to struggle anymore. I step back, I ask that you prepare the way. I thank you for the wisdom to know when to push and the wisdom to know when to move myself out of your way.

It is not by any might or power of my own that anything good comes my way, but it by your Spirit. I will not fear or panic, my world is in your hands.

Thank you for your continued faithfulness and favor in my life. Because of this, I can say, "I am a strong woman of faith!"

Father, thank you for fighting my battles, I know you always win. I refuse to hold malice. I remember Jesus on the cross asking you to forgive the men that were wanting him dead, because they didn't know what they were doing, it is not always easy, but I am determined to say, "I forgive."

I thank you that I have planted good seeds in my garden of life and according to your Word; I will reap a bountiful crop. I will reap faith, knowledge, wisdom, and I will reap a harvest of your bountiful goods that I need in this life. All parts of my being are in your hands. I am expecting double recompense because your word says it.

I decree these things in Jesus' name,

With love,
Your Woman Of Strong Faith

Psalms 40:5 Many, O LORD, my God, are your wonderful works which you have done...........they are more than can be numbered.

The Waiting

My Daughter,

While you are in the waiting, allow this perfect opportunity to grow your faith. We are establishing a trust relationship. You will grow to love my faithfulness. Your trust in me will grow in this type of soil.

Here is your reward. Hold out your hand to me and I will give you manna that is straight from my throne. You have never tasted the richness of this bread. Eat your fill, because I have plenty to spare.

Your heart is now beating as my heart. I want my people encouraged, healed and set free. I have given you my heart and I am anointing your words with great power and authority.

You have passed this most recent test. I am your friend and I have helped you. You were not aware that this was a test, but by this test, you were sanded and refined.

You will cease your crying. Let me prove myself faithful to you. I will always lovingly care for you.

Do not worry about what will become of you, I have your life in my hands. As long as you obey my instructions, a wonderful way will be made for you.

Faithfully,
Loving Father

Dear Faithful, Loving Father,

Thank you for this time of growth, I have seen your faithfulness and love during this time of waiting for promises to be fulfilled.

Here is my hand, Lord. Thank you for the good taste of your manna. I desire everything that you have for me.

Thank you for sharing with me your heart, I welcome the anointing of the Holy Spirit, and I open my heart to you, fill me up.

You have lovingly cared for me; I will cease from crying about the past and worrying about the future, for you are my future.

My desire is to please you in every moment of my life. In Jesus' name I pray.

I will cease my worrying about my future. I am in your hands. Help me to obey your instructions so that I may be pleasing to you. My whole heart's desire is to please you.

I look forward to seeing the fulfillment of your promises in my life and for the provisions you have planned for me.

I am yours,
Your Refined Daughter

Psalms 40:8 I delight to do thy will, O my God; yes, thy law is written on my heart.

Expect Miracles

Expectant Daughter,

Expect miracles every day, look expectantly as you pray. The enemy has attacked savagely, but I will redeem everything back to you.

The parade will now begin. I am speaking of the people that I have sent to you with my Word in their mouth. They will come and stand before you from near and far. My message to you will ring loudly in your ears.

The answer to all of life's problems is, standing upon my promises that cannot fail. Ask for what you need. I flow through you, you are my vessel, and the one I want to bless. See yourself as I see you, one highly anointed by me. Begin to ask for angels to minister to you and your family.

Ask everyday, and blessings will begin to pour. Your heart must be opened to me, make your requests to me.

The amount of finances now available for your use is but a small measure of what I can place into your hands. Use your faith and see what I will do for you. Ask for the double portion of my Spirit and I will bless you.

Test the spirits to see if they are of me; and fear no man; for I am greater than any man. Keep your thoughts close to your heart allow me to work the necessary deliverance and healing. There are some things that I will speak softly to you and they are for your ears only. At times there will be things I will allow you to share with others.

Souls are more important than you always digging deep within your own heart.

When you are continually look inward, you miss seeing the needs of others.

You are correct in saying that I can heal you, as you travel through the sea of needs in hurting people that are scattered throughout the world.

Blessings,
Your Faithful Father

Dear Faithful Father,

Father, I expect your miracles every day. I receive the counsel of the Most High. I stand upon your promises, because you are faithful and true. Thank you for your Spirit. I receive every spiritual blessing Christ died to give to me.

I no longer look at myself through my clouded, tear filled eyes, but I believe the things that you say concerning me. You have perfect eyesight.

Angels, in Jesus' name, I release you to gather everything that God has promised to his children, I make all my requests unto you Lord and you answer when I call.

Father, I now ask for, and receive, the double-portion anointing of your Spirit, and receive all of the blessings you have for me.

I will fear no man. Fear has no place in me. I love and respect the Lord and his Word. I test everything spoken to me by the Holy Scriptures. Your Word is quick, alive, and powerful, I reject error and I embrace God's truth.

Father, provide wisdom to guide me in all things.

I determine in my heart to reach out to hurting souls, believing you will heal me as I go.

I pray in Jesus' name,

About Your work,
Your Double-Portion Daughter.

> **Psalms 42:8 The LORD will command his loving-kindness in the daytime, and in the night his song shall be with me...**

Give Your Resources

Dear Precious Daughter,

Give your resources to me and I will make you prosperous. Trust me completely, even though you have been ripped and torn more times than you would like to admit. Many of my children died still believing my promises, you will see everything more clearly one day.

There is no human being needed to help fulfill my promises. I can do all things by myself. I now reveal my thoughts regarding those that have allowed the enemy to strike you.

People do not take my word seriously about harming my servants. Sit down, watch and see what becomes of those who harm the servants of God.

You have served me and attempted to do what is right in my eyes. I will jealously defend you. The broken places are hindering you from going forth into my fields of harvest. Whatever needs done to help you, I will do.

Time is ticking away and the hour is late. I have places to send you and these attacks and distractions must be dealt with. I want you to know how much I love you and how much I have need of you in my fields .

The enemy has had a long period of deceiving and devouring you; now the time of payback is here. There will be a swift moving of my hand against your enemies. The Devil will wish he had passed on by your dwelling.

My blessings will rest upon you, others will not be so fortunate. I do not bless sin.

My purposes and plans have been hindered. I remove obstacles in my path.

Mercy and Justice,
From Father

Dear Merciful Father,

I give you my resources and thanks for prosperity. I receive prosperity of heart, health, mind, and finances.

I stand upon your promises and I refuse to let go of one of them. Thank you for helping me by your power alone. Thank you for defending me.

Remember mercy with judgment to those that the enemy has used against me. The enemy blinded them, I forgive them and I ask you to forgive them as well.

Thank you for doing whatever is necessary to get me back upon my feet so I can be happy and busy doing the work of the ministry. The hour is late and, because of this, you are moving swiftly with healing in your wings.

In the name of Jesus, I am determined to make the enemy return everything that has been stolen. I receive your blessings today. Thank you for clearing my pathway by your Spirit.

I thank you in Jesus' name,

Humbly,
Your Defended Daughter

Psalms 41:1-2 Blessed is he that considers the poor; the LORD will deliver him in time of trouble. The LORD will preserve him, and keep him alive; and he shall be blessed upon the earth.........

Depend on My Love

Dear Dependent Daughter,

You are in a place where you must depend upon my love. I have set you apart to complete a closeness with me that is necessary to produce the fruit for the ministry that I have called you to.

This season will come to a close and like springtime brings forth-new flowers from the ground, so the next season will cause you to bloom and prosper. The fragrance from your life will enrich those to whom I will send you.

Your faith has been challenged, your mind has been assaulted, and your body is yearning for rest without the pain. Allow me to care for you.

Do not fear the future, for I am your future. My resources are more than you can imagine. Simply experience each new day with joy, ask my counsel and direction, and step by step I will heal everything in your life.

I am a prayer answering God, and I am full of loving compassion. My heart has ached for the turmoil and pain that you have had to experience, but I say to you that I will make it all up to you.

I want you in the flow of things, to experience me in my fullness. I will encourage your heart, giving to you what is necessary for you to succeed in what I want you to do.

I know exactly where you reside, I know down to the smallest details about everything concerning my children.

My Spirit jealously guards over your life. Because of this, I have removed you from situations that would cause you harm.

Listen closely as my Spirit speaks to you.

Jealously guarding you

Dear Father,

I depend entirely upon you. Thank you for this time that you have drawn me close to your heart, it is fruit bearing time. Thank you for the new season where new things will bloom and the aroma will be sweet.

Father, I run to you and allow your presence to bring healing to my spirit, soul, and body.

You are my future; I will not fear what man will attempt to do to me. Thank you for your resources, you are strong in battle. I face each new day with faith in my heart, I receive your counsel and direction in every decision that I make.

Thank you that you answer my prayers. Thank you that you love me and want the very best for my life. Father you are loving and kind, I am touched in my heart that you would take note of my pain and suffering and promise to make it all up to me. I receive this Word from your lips in Jesus' name.

Thank you for the encouragement you give; I need it to prosper in the things that you have for me to do for you.

I thank you that you read me like a blueprint, knowing down to the most precise detail the things that are going on in my life.

Thank you for protecting me even when I didn't know I needed it. I receive your revelation knowledge today, thank you for showing me things to come.

In Jesus' name I pray,

Your Dependent Daughter

Psalms 46:1-2 God is our refuge and strength, a very timely help in trouble. Therefore we will not fear, though the earth be removed and the mountains be carried into the middle of the sea.

God Can Deliver

Beloved Daughter,

You serve a God that can deliver you out of anything large or small; therefore you are safe in my arms.

The enemy of your soul would like to shake your foundations, and change your belief systems. He tries to steal what I have planted within you.

Hold on to every promise I have made to you and sweet victory will come. Why would you worry about your tomorrows? I have them safely in my hand.

From the moment I speak a word to you, and the time of its fulfillment, the battle is on! I want you to relax and say, "The Lord has promised, that is all I need to know." "He will not fail me, nor let one of his words fall to the ground."

I have promised that no word will return to me without accomplishing what I sent it to do. My words are foolproof; I am able to do everything that I have said that I would do.

My power is completely awesome; I would like to give you a demonstration of my power and light show! Would you like for me to show you my glory and manifest my miracles before your eyes? I long to reveal myself, in all of my fullness, to my children.

My desire is for my children to know me in my power. I want their trust in my abilities to care for all of their needs.

Lovingly,
Your Delivering God

Dear Faithful, Delivering Father,

You are my God and I am trusting in you. Your power is so great that there is nothing that you cannot do and there is nothing impossible with you. I thank you for all you are fixing in my life.

Thank you for repairing my foundation, for fixing anything out of place with the things you are saying to me.

I receive your sweet victory. I hold on to my faith in you and the promises and the hope you give to me.

I am snuggled close to you, and nothing can touch me there. I no longer worry about my tomorrows, for they are in your hand.

During the period from the promise to the provision, I am relaxing in your Word. You have promised and you will deliver the things that are promised to me.

It is comforting to know that your words are foolproof, they arrive with a 100% guarantee.

I desire to see you in your power and might. Turn on the lights Lord, and let your show begin. I want to see you in your manifested miracles; I know that is your desire. My trust is in you Lord; you have the power and ability to care for every need in every person on the face of the earth.

Move by your great power this day.

In Jesus' name I pray,

Your Foundation Safe Daughter

Psalms 46:10-11 Be still and know that I am God; I will be praised among the nations, I will be praised in the earth. The LORD of hosts is with us; the God of Jacob is our shelter.

Shifting

Daughter,

There is much shifting going on in the spirit realm. Wars are being fought and won by my Spirit. As victories are secured in that realm, victories will begin to filter down into the natural realm.

My angels are fighting for my children, I am happy to give victory to my children. Continue to stand and believe in me and in my words. This is not the time to fold up your tent and go home.

I will deal with those that have harmed your soul, but at the same time, I will apply healing salve upon your wounds.

Stand still and allow me to check you out from head to toe. I have been called "The Great Physician." I have many years of practice and know just what to do for my children to cause a speedy recovery.

It is difficult for my children to imagine an abundant life, a life free of pain and concern, but there is a place in me where all striving ceases. It is a resting-place that I have provided for my believing ones. Come on into my place of healing and safety; you are welcome to enter in.

Keep your options open, stay pliable in my hands. I am shaping you into my design. Each design I create is unique in every way. You are one of my masterpieces in the making. Yield to me.

I have special things I desire to accomplish in every life, do not fight the process. Just as the clay is applied to the potter's wheel and offers no resistance to change, so you too must relax and allow me to shape and make you into a beautiful vessel, one that pleases me.

I will set the finished product on a stage for all to see.

Carefully,
From Father

Dear Careful Father,

Father I thank you that your power far exceeds the power of the enemy. I thank you that victories are being won by your Spirit every moment of every day. As I awaken each morning I look for results to appear in the areas of war where I have believed for your victory.

Your angels fight every day to bring answers to the prayers of your children; I am one that will reap the benefits of the angels' successes in battle. I continue to stand in faith that you do answer my prayers. I believe the promises you have made to me; I won't give up and quit.

Your healing salve is what I need for the battle wounds, thank you for applying it liberally to the injured areas. I know you as my "Great Physician," you know exactly what is wrong and how to bring a quick and complete fix.

I release those that have harmed me, and I place them in your hands. You will do what is best in these situations.

Father, I want to enter this place where all striving ceases, show me how. I need your resting place; I want your healing and safety in my life.

Father, I remain pliable in your hands; make me into your image.

I yield to the work you wish to do in my life; I want to be like the clay that offers no resistance to your shaping.

When I look into a mirror I want to see your reflection.

In Jesus' name I pray,

Wonderfully made,
Your Work In Progress

Psalms 50:15 And call on me in the day of trouble: I will deliver you, and you will glorify ME.

Fame and Fortune

Beloved Daughter,

Fame and fortune cannot guarantee success. True success happens from within the heart of man. Without me, there is no lasting happiness. No amount of idol worship and financial gain can bring help to a broken life. I can give blessings in this life and add no sorrow to them.

Open up your heart this day and experience me. I have so much more to offer than you have ever experienced.

Today's generation expects instant gratification. When you pray you must believe that the answers are coming, and act as if they are already in your possession.

One day you will look down at your hands and they shall be filled with the results of what you believed for. Faith can be an exciting venture.

I want my people to be filled with hope, not turned away without answers to their prayers. It is when answers come that I am glorified in my people. My abilities and my power to deliver have not changed. I still do today what no other power can do. I long to be actively involved in the lives of my people.

Many trials come in life, but I can always deliver and save, even in the most bizarre situations. In your present situation of difficulty, I am busy at work. I began even before the storm approached land. I have been working continually. Flesh cannot see all that I am doing, but with faith in me, you know I am doing good things for you.

Life is a series of pieces put together one moment at a time. The picture isn't completely visible or understood until the last piece is added. In the meantime, people of faith wait patiently for the outcome of their situations to be resolved.

When my children know my abilities and my love, they can rest and trust me all of the way. You can say, "I will trust in the Lord and His unfailing love."

Faithfully,
Your Father

Dear Faithful Father,

I thank you for true riches. My heart has been touched by your love and I now have so many precious deposits within my spirit. Thank you for healing my broken life. I receive your blessings and understand that you add no sorrow to them.

I have opened my heart to you, Lord; I want to experience your life with all of its fullness.

I believe I have received those things that I have prayed for. Thank you that you are a prayer-answering God. I welcome you into my life, take over every aspect of it. In my spirit, I look at my hands and see the treasures, both tangible and non-tangible that you have promised. I know the wars are won first in the spirit before they are seen in the visible realm.

Father, even wild and crazy situations are no problem with you. They will all bow in your presence. You are a Mighty God.

I am a woman of faith, and I expectantly watch for your answers to come. You will heal the brokenness of my life. You will supply my need. You will make the dreams that have been placed within me become real in the here and now.

Jesus, you are so kind and loving, you are the exact image of my Heavenly Father. Lord I do trust in your unfailing love.

I thank you in Jesus' name,

Your Wealthy Daughter

> **Psalms 57:9-11 I will praise thee, O LORD, among the people; I will sing to You among the nations; for your mercy and truth reach up to heaven; You are exalted above the heavens and Your glory is above the earth.**

My Spirit

Daughter,

In the waiting time for my promises to come to you, my Holy Spirit will show you how to remain proactive in your faith. You are not to sit doing nothing, twiddling your thumbs, waiting for me to do all of the work.

It is true that the battle is mine, but your part is to actively believe me for my victories to become yours. As these victories come, we will rejoice together.

I am not struggling and worrying about how I can bring resolution to this mountain that is defying your God. Giants fall on their face before my presence.

Sometimes there is a struggle that rages within your mind, but I want you to know that I have everything under my control.

Man is no match for me. How can flesh win over its maker? This will never happen!

Everything I say comes to pass. Within the seed of what I speak, lies the power of a Almighty God to bring about its fulfillment.

Once my Word leaves my lips, things begin to happen. Those things contrary to my will begin to remove themselves from my pathway. Nothing can stand in the wake of my Word. All must make way for the entrance of my Word. My Word is life and power.

Believe!

Patiently,
Your Warrior Father

Dearest Warrior Father,

I thank you for revealing to me how to stay in faith. I am now aware that my portion of the assignment is to actively believe you will do everything that you have said you would do for me. I am so thankful that you are so great and powerful that giants fall on their face before your feet.

Thank you for controlling the events of my life. Thank you that flesh never wins. Every word that you speak, has within its core, the power to bring forth that which you have spoken.

I thank you for speaking into my life, and I believe those things were released for me the moment the words left your lips.

I believe that things that stood in the way of your Word are now running for cover.

Lord, concern yourself no more as to whether I will stand and believe your Word. It is already settled in my heart, I am standing strong in you. I will stand until I see the results of those things you have spoken to me.

Because of my trust in your Word, I am now enjoying each moment as if I was resting upon pillows and coverings filled with exquisite feathers.

I am under our wings and feathers and I am comfortable and safe. It now has become a smooth easy flight, thank you Lord.

I am so relieved to be rid of the fear and unbelief, now good things can come my way.

In Jesus' name I pray,

> Standing strong,
> Your Faith Daughter

Psalms 57:1 Be merciful to me LORD, for my soul trusts in You. I will make my refuge in the shadow of your wings until these sorrows pass.

Enemies of Faith

Warrior Daughter,

I don't stand wringing my hands in despair, wondering about the outcome of your deliverance. I know what I am going to do.

My biggest concern is whether you will allow me to impart this Word into your life, and if you will take your stand with me and trust in my Word to you, regardless of circumstances or time frame.

How long you remain in the battle can effect the quality of the campaign. The fight can be one of ease or one of great struggle.

When I have already spoken and declared the battle's outcome, the journey can be one of ease. Often my people allow carnal thinking to enter, and the ensuing battle becomes one of stress and fatigue. This is all so unnecessary. The battle is not yours, it is mine. I had spoken my Word to give my child a smooth easy fight, but you, the warrior, entered into the fight with fear and unbelief.

Can anything good come from these two enemies of faith?

Waiting Father

Dear Father,

I am ashamed that sometimes I neglect to exercise faith. I know you do not lie. Your words are alive. Every word you speak has life and will come to pass.

My battle has gone on for an extended period of time. How many times must I be reminded that it is your battle, not mine.

I see why I have lingered so long on the battlefield. It is because I am trying to give the commands and manage the outcome.

Father, create in me a clean heart and a clear mind so I can be faithful to your Words to me. I need to rest in your arms while you do battle for me. The battle makes me so weary.

I lay down my carnal weapons and pick up the shield of faith and the sword of the Spirit, which is the Word of God. I put on the whole armor, Father, Commander. lead... I will follow.

In Jesus' name I pray and trust,

Lovingly,
Your Wise Daughter

Psalms 59:16 I will sing of your power. Yes, I will sing songs aloud about your mercy in the morning and your defense in the day of trouble.

When It Is Time

Dear Ready Daughter,

When I decide it is time to move, things happen quickly. The field of your heart has been prepared, the seed has been planted, the rains have come and gone and the harvest time is here.

The lean years are behind you, it is time to prosper. I am never late, always on time. It is now that you will truly appreciate my goodness, for you have tasted the bitter herbs. Look to no man or woman, look into my eyes and see my love for you there.

Now you have learned the importance of obedience. You will follow my direction, and greener pastures will be located. There will be quiet days for your refreshing. Let my Words come slowly and smoothly.

Follow through on the things that I advise you to do. Be diligent to listen to all of my instructions. Develop your spirit to hear in the small things, and in the big things.

My Spirit will guide you around all of the pitfalls of the enemy. I will show you where to place your feet. I know everything about everything. Obey the prompting of my Spirit.

I am beginning to rain finances down upon your head! You will sing, "Its raining money!" Out of nowhere will it come, from near and far will it come. The faucet has been opened.

Give everything to me today, there is nothing you can fix. I am the repairer of all broken things.

Look for my miracles; they are all along the road.

Generously,
Your Loving Father

Dear Loving Father,

You are in control of my life. I thank you for moving speedily for me. I know it only takes a moment for things to change for the better when you are in charge.

Thank you for the time you spent in preparation on the ground of my spirit. Thank you for the seeds of your Word. Thank you for the tilling and weeding. It hurt sometimes, but I can see the benefits now. Thank you for harvest time. I am looking to you for all of my needs, and I am glad that you love me.

Father, I will be diligent to listen to your instructions and do what you ask of me. I want to be obedient in the small things and the big things.

Thank you for your guidance and safety. Your eye sees it all, and I can trust you. You know my need. You know the plan for my life. You know the little side roads I have taken outside of your will. You knew how to make the errant path merge again into the main road of your will. Thank you for being the navigator of my life.

Father, I thank you for the financial increase. I am thankful that you delight in the prosperity of your servants.

I am resting in the knowledge that you can repair everything that is broken in my life.

My eyes are open to see your miracles all along the path you have chosen for me.

In Jesus' name I pray,

Thankfully,
Your Blessed Daughter

Psalms 72:18 Blessed is the LORD God, who only does wondrous things.

<u>Fatigue</u>

Daughter,

There are days when fatigue, with all of its weariness and uncertainty, tries to settle upon you. Impatience tries to settle as well. This is put a portion of the mixture of things that contribute to a hard day.

It is in the hard days that you prove your faith. You cannot change your situations, I am the only one who can. I've heard all of your prayers.

Look back, have I not provided for you each day and night?I do not always put my children up in the finest places. Remember the manger? But, I do provide. My provision is always within a master plan. I plan the deliverance for my children.

Stand strong in the power of my might. Pray and believe, that is your part, and then I will do my part.

Discouragement tries to assail my children. Remember the"dis" is "a removal of" courage. I am strong in my people, allow that power and strength to come forth for it is within you. There is a deep cleansing going on in you. I've covered your back, and all the way around you.

A warrior is within you, not a defeated weakling! Allow me to flow out to the world that needs a savior and a deliverer. I need trained warriors in my harvest fields.

Roll up your sleeves, get ready to get down in the ditches and bring out those who are bound and dying. I will anoint you to do this. Your enthusiasm for me will inspire hope and courage in others.

You have released yourself into my hands, giving me free rein in your life. All that I require of you is that you fulfill the purpose that I designed you for. There is a specific destiny for every child of mine. Let me bring you to that place.

It would be an impossible journey without my help. I do give my help to my children and things will improve and the sun will shine brighter as they follow my directions. Why is that so difficult for you to believe? You know that I do not lie.

Patiently,
Your Commander Father

Father,

Thank you for revealing to me the particulars regarding why I feel like I do. Now I will guard against becoming too tired, being impatient and allowing uncertainty about my future to cause stress in my life.

My faith is proved when I stand strong in those times of trouble when I can't see with my eyes what you are doing for me. I am totally dependent upon you lord, you are the only one that can correct these problem areas in my life.

Thank you for hearing all of the prayers that have been prayed for my help. I stand strong in the name of Jesus, believing you for great deliverance. I have prayed, and now I believe that those things I have asked of you will be done.

Thank you for returning my courage to me, you are my high tower, my rock, and my fortress. Because you live inside of me, I am strong in the power of your might. I am a mighty warrior, and not a defeated believer. Thank you for the cleansing power of the blood of Jesus. I am covered on every side of my life.

Father, I am reporting for duty in your army, what do you have for me to do? I will get into the ditches and bring out the wounded since that is what you are asking of me.

Thank you for the anointing of the Holy Spirit, I ask for more of your zeal and enthusiasm. Here is my hand Lord, take me to the place where I fit in this army. It is my desire to hear your voice, follow your directions and move by your Spirit. I long to see that gorgeous sunshine; so I put away unbelief and doubt. Father I thank you that you always tell the truth.

Your Encouraged Daughter

> **Psalms 73:28 It is good for me to draw near to God; I have put my trust in the LORD God.**

Holding You

Daughter,

I am the one holding you steady and secure. No man or woman can take credit for what I am doing in your life. I am the one speaking great and marvelous things for your ears to hear. You must hold on to and trust in what I say to you. The enemy can move upon friends, family, or enemies to spread his poison potion of doubt, fear, and unbelief.

Just know that I have ample ability to whisper into your ear in such a way that you will know that I am speaking to you.

The devil knows what has worked in the past, and he will mix the same brew on your current set of problems. Now is the time to say, "no more! I will not fear what man may say, for I have the Word of the Lord still echoing in my ears, and I choose to believe what he has said to me!"

Following this course requires deliberate courage, and the strength of determination and patience.

Wipe out the former failures, you can start again. Know that I have complete rule and dominion in this world, for this world is mine, made by my hands.

I would now like to talk to you about the power that is in letting go. There are many examples in your own life where I brought you to this place, and you saw my hand move for you every time. Pray and ask me to help you release things into my hands.

In every battle there is a release valve where your fingers must let go, the switch is released, thus causing your hands to be removed in one swift action.

It is then that I can move unhindered, bringing forth the best answers imaginable.

Awaiting your release,
Loving Father

Dear Loving Father,

I thank you for your strong steady hand upon my life. When your promises show up on my doorstep, no one but you can take credit for the miracles I have received.

My trust is in the Word of the Lord, for you do not lie!

I shut my ears to the whispers of the enemy. My ears are hearing all that you Lord, have promised me; I believe you, Father. I am yielding myself to deliberate courage, determination, and patience.

Today is a new beginning, all of my past failures are put away, and I now start anew.

The earth is the Lord's and the fullness thereof, and all of them who dwell upon the earth.

Lord it's all yours, even all the silver and all of the gold belongs to you.

The cattle on a thousand hills are yours too. How awesomely prosperous you are!

Your Word says I am a joint heir with Jesus, so all of the above is shared with me as well. You always take wonderful care of your children. Today I am letting go… my life is in your hands. Let me experience the power that is in letting go of things. Help me to let go.

I place my fingers on the release switch, and now your hands are in control.

Now we can get this show on the road!

In Jesus' name I pray,

Trusting,
Joint-Heir Daughter

> **Psalms 80:19 Restore us, O LORD God of hosts; cause thy face to shine, and we shall be saved.**

Your Purpose

Daughter,

Pursue your passion and then you will find your purpose. This is a statement I want you to ponder.

First, let me reveal your passion to you. It has been kicked under tons of troubles, and doesn't seem worth the effort that it would take to dig it out and dust it off. These were things that once thrilled your heart, now the thrill is gone. Where is it lying buried?

I know exactly where it is located and what needs to be done to get it back in operation. There is a trunk tucked away with treasures that were for your enjoyment.

In this trunk lies buried hopes, dreams, joy, and peace. These, you once wore like a garment, there was a robe and a mantle.

Take them out again. They are not too small or too large. You will find that the seasons you have endured since last you thought of them have prepared you to wear them with more maturity.

Don't you think you should examine the trunk? We could remove all of these items. They will restore your former passion.

Let's sort through this together, I know exactly what you need and what will bring about great change as you begin wearing the garments that are tucked away.

I have great delight in your re-discovery of your passions. There, you will re-discover your purpose, the one I intended for you; the one that was side-tracked by worry, grief, and circumstances.

Something good is heading your way. I know just the tonic that you need, let me encourage you this day. Keep your faith held tightly, do not allow it to be stolen, you will see many answers to prayer.

Delightfully,
Your Loving Father

Dear Loving Father,

I thank you for anointed men and women of God who pursue their passion and find their purpose. I want to be such as these.

I ponder everything you say to me, always desiring to hear your voice.

It is true that I have allowed my passion for life to be hidden and buried, out of sight, and nearly out of mind.

Thank you, Father, that you are now removing the ton of things blocking out my passion, and once again I will arise with the zeal of the Lord. This is my season to recover all, so I look to you in faith, believing for all things to be returned to me.

Father, as you begin speaking to me of my passion, I want to be adorned with the garments that please you. Let me wear them with dignity and maturity. Parents love buying and making garments for their children. Parents want the garments to fit. I feel that I am now ready to wear these garments with maturity. You are a wonderful, Mighty God. I feel like a child, trying on new outfits and modeling them for the delight of her Father. I feel so loved.

Thank you for the remedy that is specially made to cure all of my troubles. I hold to my faith with all of my might, I'll not let go, and I will see many answers to prayer.

In Jesus' name I pray,

Getting Dressed,
Your Believing Daughter

> **Psalms 89:1 I will sing of the mercies of the LORD forever; I will make known Your faithfulness to all generations.**

Undeserved

Daughter,

Every person experiences things that are undeserving and unfair. When these things come, you must square your shoulders, and take my hand.

This is a time when you must believe my Word, let me guide you and bring about the deliverance that you seek.

Just as my angel shut the mouth of the lions for Daniel, and I rescued him from certain death, I am the same today and rescue all whose heart is right before me.

Sickness and disease must bow in my presence. I have not lost my power to deliver. I deliver daily, it just doesn't always make the front page.

I am strong! I deliver my believing ones.

These enemies that have arisen against you shall be struck down. You rest while I work and when it is finished; you will see the reward of the wicked.

Your eyes shall see their devastation, but it shall not come near you.

Delivering,
Strong Father

Dear Strong Father,

At your command, I stand up, square my shoulders, and grasp your hand, for your hand guides me out of all my troubles.

I am thankful that you have not lost any of your power. The same God that delivered godly people in times past will deliver me.

The things that you do for me make front-page placement in my testimony. Every day you do marvelous things. You will strike down my enemies, those wicked spirits that perpetrate evil against me.

I will be given a front row seat and watch your awesome "Power and Light Show."

Thank you for your protection.

I pray in Jesus' name,

Still standing,
Your Front Page Daughter

Psalms 91:1-2 I will live in the secret pace of the Most High God will stay safely hidden under His shadow. I will say of the LORD, He is my refuge and fortress; my God; and I will trust Him.

Tell My People

Dear Daughter,

Tell my people that I am soon to return, and not to let the Son catch them sleeping.

I am coming for a Bride that is awake, one alert, listening for my voice.

Tell my Bride to make herself ready, I desire her to be clean and well groomed as she makes her arrival to her new home.

It is a lovely dwelling place, more beautiful than she can imagine. She will be loved and all of her cares will vanish.

She will live in this home permanently, never again to experience pain or loss.

Grace and Mercy,
Your Loving Father

Dear Loving Father,

I will tell others of your soon return to this earth. I will encourage them to keep oil in their lamps so that when their Heavenly Bridegroom comes, they will be ready to see him.

As a member of the body of Christ, I keep check upon my own heart and ways.

Cleanse me from all unrighteousness, ironing out all of my wrinkles, spots and blemishes. I desire to be prepared for the trip of a lifetime!

Thank you, Father, for the promise of this wonderful new home where all pain and sorrows are wiped away.

My eyes and ears are open to your Word to me today. I long to please you in all of my ways.

In Jesus' name I pray.

Awaiting your arrival,
Your Bride

Psalm 90:12 So teach us to number our days that we may apply our hearts to wisdom.

Help Is on the Way

Dear Daughter,

I am sending to you those that I wish to be a part of the work that I have commissioned you to do. They will pour water upon your hands and feet, and many will bring to you treasures from my provisional house of plenty.

Angels are arriving with these things as well. Some things had been sidetracked, held up in traffic, so to speak, but I am taking care of these things.

Daughter, my angels are real; they are not imaginary. They work hard for me. They are strong in battle, overcoming the might of your strongest enemies. Watch them fight for you. This will be evidenced by you in what you will see with your eyes.

I have listened to your words, and now the flow of goods is heading toward your dwelling. Provisions for the journey are being provided. Watch for my gifts!

From Father

Dear Father,

I thank you for sending individuals that have been called to help with the work you have called me to do. Thank you that they will be a blessing to my life and I pray that you will make me a blessing to them as well.

Thank you for those delayed blessings, the ones held up by spirit traffic, your angels have won that battle for me. You hear me when I pray, so I can rest my heart in knowing that your answers are on the way. I believe your angels are real because the Holy Scriptures tell me this is true. I have sincere appreciation for the work that you instruct them to do for me. Your angels excel in strength and have never lost a battle, I am so glad they are fighting for me. I receive your promised provisions right now. In Jesus' name I pray,

Watching and Waiting,
Your Appreciative Daughter

Psalm91:11-12   For He shall give His angels charge over you, to keep you in all your ways. They shall hold you up in their hands to keep you from harm.

The Medical Community

Dear Daughter,

The medical community is aware of the dangerous effects of long term use of prescribed medicines. They advise and warn patients of these dangers. For example, too much of an antibiotic will cause resistance to the infection that it was meant to cure. After a period of time, the usefulness of the medication is lost.

My Word is a medicine for the body, mind and spirit. When I deal with people about areas needing a cleansing, if they continually turn their head and refuse to hear my Word of correction, soon my voice begins to sound like a distant echo.

The heart has been hardened the conscience seared, and a total disregard for my counsel sets in. A constant yielding to sin causes sick bodies, troubled minds, and broken spirits.

Instruct my children to heed My Word.

Tenderly,
The Great Physician

Dear Great Physician,

Your Word is medicine and health to all my flesh; it cleanses the soul and spirit of man.

In Jesus' name, I will never turn my head and walk away from your dealings with me. I will yield to the correction of your Word.

I want my heart to remain sensitive to your Spirit, my mind to be tender toward your Word and my spirit alive to hear the things you say to me. Thank you for the wisdom to constantly yield to your Spirit.

Thank you that I recognize the rod of correction when it is presented to me. I yield to your will and your way.

It is in Jesus' name I pray,

Yielding,
Your Corrected Daughter

Psalms 97:6   **The heavens declare His righteousness, and all the people see His glory.**

Woman of Faith

Dear Faith-Walking Daughter,

A woman of faith walks defying the obstacles, swinging her sword, and she has a song of praise upon her lips.

Lift your eyes beyond these temporary problems, for these problems will soon be gone. I will wipe them away by the breath of my mouth.

Begin to sing and make music in your heart for the victory that is already guaranteed. I cannot be told what to do, but I can be moved by your love, trust and faith. You have been growing even though you can't see or feel it. I am happy with your progress.

It is still necessary for you to release problems to me. Fear keeps you from trusting me with the outcome. The devil can only win if you let him. Stand strong, victory is straight ahead. You are pressing through to the finish line. This trial is nearly over.

The enemy is painting you pictures of how the ending of this will be. He knows nothing that I am doing. I want you to trust the picture I am giving to you. Trust your spirit, I speak to you there. I will help you separate truth from fiction. I have been teaching you to trust me more.

Bad things do not have to keep happening; I can call an end to this recurring thievery! Never back up on the ministry again; work while daylight hours are still available.

Today I spared two special ones that you love, praise me for being there when help was needed. Be thankful for everything you can think of. I love a thankful heart. Stop fighting in your own strength against your circumstances. Learn to depend upon my love and rest, rest, rest.

My soldiers fight with my Word, not with their emotions.

Stand Strong!
From Father

Dear Father,

I am your woman of faith. I have a song of praise upon my lips, and I am swinging the sword of the Lord. In the name of Jesus, I defy everything that even thinks about standing in my way!

Thank you for your breath that is wiping away these temporary troubles. I receive my guaranteed victory now.

I thank you that you find me pleasing in your eyes, and I thank you for the growth you have given to me.

By your grace, I no longer look with fear regarding my future, I refuse to look at the devil's snapshot, but I am continually looking to the face of the architect of the entire universe.

Thank you for revelation knowledge, and for the halting of the recurring bad experiences I have encountered.

I praise you for your protection upon my life, also for the lives of my loved ones. I am now standing in the strength of the Lord. Thank you for your love and mercy.

I thank you that I now fight the battles with your Word, and my emotions have received their discharge papers from active duty!

I pray all of this in Jesus' name,

Resting,
Your Warrior Daughter

Psalms 100:5   For the LORD is good; His mercy is forevermore, and His truth will last for all generations.

Allow Me

Daughter,

Allow me free access to everything in your life and I will do exploits. Would you like to see me perform miracles? Just watch and be thrilled. I am your redeemer, savior, and friend, I will now move for you.

Recently someone said that God knows how to make a stubborn person say "uncle." This is a true statement spoken for your ears to hear.

Stop and think about the men and women that I have dealt with throughout history, none conquered me, but I caused them to yield or face the consequences. I can do the same with that one that is like a thorn in your flesh.

Daughter, when I begin speaking to you about a particular area of promise, act upon it with your faith. Use these words of mine to "flip on the switch of faith" and watch the heavy equipment roll in and begin clearing a pathway for you to travel.

Allow me to have total care and control of your life. It will cause you to lead a blessed life.

It is past time for you to experience and enjoy a secure, loving, and safe life. I intend to see that you possess it. Weep no more, for my command has already been given and the angels are even now carrying out my orders regarding your well being.

You will sing again, this time from a heart that is truly full. Your heart will be one that is thankful for a new season, one filled with happiness and joy.

I have a place of abundance for you. Let me take you there. Many pleasant surprises await you. Come away with me, I will take you there.

Blessings,
Your Protecting Father

Dear Protecting Father,

I invite you into my life with full access to every compartment.

Thank you that you are my redeemer, savior, and friend, and you are moving for me.

I choose to be a child that yields to your will immediately. I have switched my faith button to the "on" position and am watching for your emergency equipment to roll in. I thank you because I have given full control to you that I lead a blessed life.

It is exciting to know that your command has already been issued for my well being. Right now I open my mouth and begin to sing with a heart that is full of joy and peace.

I embrace this new season that you have given to me. Thank you for this new place of abundance, I welcome the pleasant surprises I have found here.

In the name of Jesus I pray,

Yielding Daughter

> **Psalms 91:9-10 Because I made the Lord my refuge, I made the Most High my constant dwelling place, no evils shall befall me nor any plague come near my dwelling. HE will give his angels charge over me to keep me.**

Ready?

Dear Prepared Daughter,

Are you ready to go for me? Open wide the door of trust and watch me take you into places you never dreamed possible.

When you have doubts regarding an invitation, slow down, step back, and continue praying. My leading is clear and deliberate, you will have a settling in your spirit as to what I want you to do.

You absolutely cannot make anything happen .Your life is in my hands, and your welfare is my concern, not yours.

I desire to bless your life; I am now re-dressing you for service. I need you, and I will make others want those things that I have placed inside of you.

If my door opens, walk through it. If not, stand still, love me, and wait.

On a city street there are shops lining both sides of the street. Things that are displayed in the windows are meant to attract and sometimes seduce. In life, sometimes things that look good are meant to snare your soul. Always ask my advice and counsel regarding your purchases.

Today pack up all your troubles and give them to me. Rest is coming your way.

Rest-Giving Father

Dear Rest-Giving Father,

With your help and grace, I will work for you. I choose today to begin trusting you with my life.

Thank you for all of the wonderful places you will take me, I am happy to know that your direction will be clear and precise.

I am relieved that I am in your care and my welfare is your concern. I have learned that you love to bless your children, and I am excited to experience all you are bringing into my life.

The new garments for serving you are sincerely appreciated. Thank you for deciding what I wear well, you always choose the very best for me.

By your grace, I will only walk through the doors that you open. I will be still and wait upon your direction.

Lord, many times I felt as if no one had any interest in me, but now I hear you say that you want me. Thank you, thank you, and thank you again.

Father, I am listening to your warnings about things that would attempt to snare my soul. I ask your advice and counsel about what is safe for me.

My bags are packed Lord and I now give to you all of my troubles. I'm glad to be rid of them.

In Jesus' name I pray,

Awaiting Your Rest,
Your Willing Daughter

> **Psalms 91:13-16   I shall walk on the lion and the snake. Because I have loved my LORD and I have known His name, He will deliver me and set me on high. When I call upon God, he will hear and answer me. He will be with me in trouble. He will honor me and satisfy me with long life.**

Believing and Receiving

Daughter,

Believing and receiving, what a concept! So simple, and yet my people make it so complex. A lack of patience and a spirit of doubt - these two, keep answers from manifesting.

Defy the circumstances and the circumstances will change! You have my Word on that! It cannot be a thing of the mind. It must be a believing in the heart. It is simply accepting my Word regardless of what you see, feel, or think.

I am a prayer answering Father, and I yearn to give my children the desires of their heart, things that I have promised them in my Word.

From the time of saying, and the time of receiving, there is always a challenge. I am watching over your faith. The enemy is in a tug of war trying to wrestle your faith from you. If you let go, you lose. The loss doesn't have to be permanent you can begin again, holding on better than before with determination and perseverance.

I will move in all of your situations. Do you trust me where you cannot see? Start speaking girl, and give me something to work with. Scripture works for all of my children. You just need to be a strong soldier and be determined to get all I have promised you.
No one else can do this for you, you must do it.

I will work out the details. Doubts will present themselves to you. Just simply say, "I believe that I have already received what I have prayed for!" As you dare to believe me, the importance of your words will become more evident to you. As you take your stand, and I see your faith, the pathway will be cleared and the answer will come. When my children dare to doubt their doubts, they received miracles!

Steadfast Father

Dear Prayer Answering Father,

Father, right now I believe that I receive all that I have asked of you those things that are in your will. I believe that your will is good for me, and your will always brings true happiness. New and wonderful things are coming my way.

I know you give me the desires of my heart. I receive the desires of my heart. I will not give up, I am holding on to my faith. I trust you with every situation in my life. I will speak your Word and see your miracles. I defy the ugly circumstances of my life in the name of Jesus. My circumstances will change for my good.

My determination to stand upon your Word is not based on a thing of the mind, but upon a knowing in my heart. What I see, think, or feel will not move me. I will exercise faith vision, and faith feelings. I will doubt my doubts and feed my faith on the Word of God. I will guard my faith.

Thank you for the pathway cleared and your answers arriving in style!

In Jesus' matchless name I pray,

Faith-Full Daughter

Psalms 98:1 Sing a new song to the Lord for he has done marvelous things. His holiness and strength have brought the victory.

Share The Good News

Daughter,

Calls will begin to come for you to share my Good News. I have placed people in strategic locations where I desire to display my awesome power. Listen carefully, I will speak to you regarding where you are to go.

You and I talk with each other more than you realize. Your spirit cries out to me and I respond to those cries.

I am in the process of breaking down and rebuilding some things in your life. My touch will reach to your hair, skin, and body and even to your wardrobe.

It is my desire for you to be filled to capacity with my Spirit, and to be filled with the confidence and zeal of the Lord.

I want you to feel like a much-loved child, one that has the full attention of her Father. I want you filled with anticipation for all the things that are coming into your life.

Be happy in me, allow my Spirit to give you great joy, for out of great joy comes great strength. Do not fear or dread what others will say they are planning for you; I will have you ready for anything.

The journey you have recently traveled has been uncertain and sad, but look where this road has led. I now have you ready to launch forward into my new anointing and my purpose.

Help my people, straighten out their wrong thinking. Give them my love and hope. I will bless you for doing this.

Walk behind me every step of the way. I will always be there. It is difficult for you to comprehend that I have so much more for you, and that I want to take you to the top, but that is what I intend to do.

The years have been long, and the battles fierce and tiring, but restoration is coming to your mind and your body. I will create restoration in both.

Surprises are awaiting you,
Strong Father

Dear Strong Father,

I thank you for the doors that are opening for me to share the Gospel of Jesus Christ.

I thank you that every time I share the good news, your power of hope, love, healing, and redemption will flow through me to your people.

I hear your voice and a stranger's voice I will not follow. Thank you for hearing and answering my prayers. I know that as you are re-building things in my life, and that I am being changed into your image. Because I am your much-loved child, I have your full attention. Thank you for attending to every detail of my life.

Thank you for the strength that you have given, I walk fearlessly through this journey called life. This new anointing you have given has prepared me for my destiny. I receive the anointing to teach your children.

I will walk with love and patience toward them and your blessing will overtake me because of my obedience to your Word.

In Jesus' name I pray,

In Obedience to the call,
Your Much-Loved Child

Psalms 100:4-5   Enter into His gates with thanksgiving, and into his courts with praise; be thankful to Him and bless his name. For the LORD is good; his mercy is everlasting, and his truth lasts for all generations.

You Need Me

Daughter,

You are being taught that you will always need me throughout your life.

Some things have you bound, however I am helping you get free. I have purposed to do this very thing.

You have acknowledged your need of me, now I will make this an easy thing for you to do.

The enemy has pressed hard against you, but I have strengthened you, and you will not be brought to the ground by these current happenings in your life.

I who made the heart can heal its broken places. I am pouring in the oil and the wine, removing all festering, cleansing the wound, and applying healing salve and dressing. I do a complete work when I restore.

This latest attack was an all -out attack meant to silence you completely. I could not let this happen. You still have places to go and people to see.

Now sleep my little prophet, my servant, with the bright shining torch.

More revelation from the Holy Spirit is coming to you.

Protectively,
Father

Dear Protective Father,

I need you in every area of my life. I thank you for your deliverance from the things that have had me bound.

I am now free, delivered by the name of Jesus and by his shed blood. I receive your power to deliver me all the days of my life. It is wonderful to know that you deliver without any effort. I receive your strengthening today. The enemy will not bring me down.

Thank you for the healing of my broken heart, for the oil and wine mixture that stopped my bleeding war torn injuries.

I have an appointment with destiny and I hold up my torch to those who are in darkness. I receive every ounce of revelation knowledge that you have promised to give me.

In Jesus' name I pray,

Your Healed Daughter

Psalms 103:1-4   Bless the Lord, O my soul, and all that is in me, bless his hold name. Bless the LORD, o my soul, and do not forget all His benefits.. He forgives all my sins and heals my diseases. He redeems my life from destruction and crowns me with loving kindness and tender mercies.

Winner's Circle

Daughter,

Do you realize there are spirits of unbelief working against you today? This is the warfare you are fighting. Stand firm in your faith. Deliverance is on the way.

The things that are bothering you matter little. I can still turn the battle around. I've been showing you examples of problems in this situation. Do you think you can deal with the issues I have pointed out?

I see the outcome of everything; I set the stage for the events of your life. I say what happens to you. The devil is not stronger than I am!

You have asked for my help in this, and I am working for you. Let my Spirit guide you through this web of deception. Even now, I am cutting you free. Trust me now with the outcome of all of this.

Will you continue working for me? Use the precious gifting I have given to you. I have removed that one that hindered your call, many are awaiting your arrival and you must not be late.

Just as a wardrobe dresser moves with great speed to help an actor into a new costume between acts, so I will move quickly for you. My angels are attending to your needs and you will be ready on time.

Think with your spiritual mind, not the natural one. I have been repairing lives for a long time. I know what to do for you, and I always do all things well.

Why would I not help you? Do you think I have brought you this far, invested so much in you, to leave you now?

I will deliver you, have no fear. I am here to help you.

Lovingly,
Your Delivering Father

Dear Delivering Father,

Thanks for letting me know what is going on. I am standing firm in my faith, taking authority over the enemy in Jesus' name. By your grace, I can do all that is required of me.

Thank you that none compares to you. Your eyes have surveyed my life, and your hand will complete any changes that are needed.

I trust you with my life for there is no one else that is trustworthy 100% of the time. My desire is to be obedient to your purpose and plans for my life.

I thank you for the preparation process, the garments that have been placed upon me by your Spirit.

I thank you for the total rebuilding of my life; your work in me has been amazing beyond compare.

Thank you for the removal of all fear, and thank you for the grace supplied to me.

I pray in Jesus' name,

Your Standing Daughter

> **Psalms 106: 1   I Praise You, Lord. I give thanks to You Lord for You are good and your mercy endures forever.**

Happy Times

Daughter,

Enjoy the happy positive things in your life. Enjoy your family, they make you happy.

I know you are tempted to give up on your dreams. You have poured out without the security of a steady income, then someone came along and in one breath, blew away what I had placed in your hands. Hope was given, then snatched away, and you were left feeling used and abused.

Many adversaries have been along your pathway, but you cannot stop now. The prize will be worth the battle. Your income in ministry has been challenged, but I will make a way for you. Things are not as they appear, for I am working behind the scenes. Count your blessings, name them one by one, then you will see what I have truly done!

Pin all of your hopes and dreams upon me. Do not look at the negative. Say with confidence, "The Lord will never leave, nor forsake me!" You were told in the beginning of this walk that you were in a war. It is a war of darkness against light and vice versa.

Some of the battles you have won. In other battles, you allowed the enemy to carry away your goods. Now stomp your foot and demand it all to be returned to you! Command the blessings of God to be released, as it is my will for you to achieve all that I have promised.

I am working in you a new strength that will refuse to bow down to the enemy. Don't apologize for standing up for yourself. It is time for your backbone to be back in place.

I am working in this, stand up and be counted. I will back you all the way. Do not think thoughts of defeat and lack, march in with force, and gather up all that belongs to you.

I have a people that will welcome and embrace you and the many gifts that I have placed within you.

Father

Dear Father,

I thank you for every good thing that you have placed in my life. I thank you for complete restoration.

I choose to look upon good things and not have a negative take on things. You will never leave or forsake me, so I have so much to be thankful for.

In Jesus' name, I command every lost item from every battle to be given back. I have pursued, I overtake, and now I recover all. Devil, you must give it up!

I feel the strength you have placed within me. My backbone is in place and I refuse to bow to the thief anymore.

I am off the mat, and back in the ring. You, Lord, are my personal trainer, and have caused me to triumph. I no longer allow thoughts of loss and defeat to harass my mind.

Thank you for those that will welcome the ministry that you have placed within me. I will allow your gifts to bless them.

In Jesus' name I pray,

Triumphantly
Your Winner's Circle Daughter

> **Psalms 107:14   He brought them out of darkness and the shadow of death, and broke their bands off. Oh, that men would praise the Lord for his goodness, and for his wonderful works...**

Dream Big Dreams

Daughter,

My Spirit is handling everything that is troubling you. We have much work to do together. I will instruct you as you walk. I will provide everything you need to be successful in the mission I have for you.

Now I am refocusing and repositioning you. I am heading you toward your promise land, I do keep my promises. I have been speaking to you for some time that I have a better life for you.

Forgetting the ways of how things happened in times past is not always an easy thing to do. Your former frame of reference is ringing in your ears, and is painted on a canvas before your eyes. I will demolish the visual, and rip out the echoes in your ears.

This is a new day. It is a day of deliverance. It is a time of moving from one dimension to another. Do not fear the move because I will hold your hand for the entire journey. I will take care of you, my servant.

Trust me for good things are in the works. I will set you in a place of permanence, a place of peace and rest. Others will long to come to this place for it shall even smell of peace. Though the vision tarries wait for it, this is my Word... This scripture demonstrates your life now. Many things I promised you years ago are getting ready to materialize. I am making you into a woman of peace, one that doesn't hurry or worry.

This is a great work I am doing in you. Listen for my voice, I will speak to you. Sometimes I will speak directly to your spirit, other times through another. I always speak through my written Word, and open doors will be speaking to you as well.

You will see my hand at work in you. The truth of my Word to you will be evident.

Why are you afraid to try? Do not ask others if you should follow me. Wherever I lead, come and pursue hard after me.

Dream big dreams for me, some former dreams failed because of people that were surrounding you. They pulled you back as you dared to dream. I placed the dreams of your heart there. Even though they didn't fully manifest back then, they are still alive and living within your heart now.

Father

Dear Father,

I thank you for taking care of every detail of my life. Thank you for the instruction that you give to me. I receive your instruction with a grateful heart.

The make over you have worked in me has made me into a secure, happy daughter. Now I can see my promised land.

Thank you for demolishing my own tiresome thoughts and the photo images of my defeated past and now I see the new photo gallery arranged by your hand. My eyes are now focused on what you reveal to me and not those things of the past.

I love this new place in you, and I plan to stay planted in this place. Thank you for the peace and the rest.

I have waited upon the Word that you spoke to me many years ago, and now I am seeing its fulfillment.

Than you for teaching me patience, I love the peace that it has produced in me.

Speak Lord, your daughter is listening.

The dream thieves have been uprooted, and I am watching my dreams come true.

I thank you in Jesus' name,

Your Dream Believer

Psalms 107:41   He sets the poor on a high place away from affliction and makes their families strong.

<u>Don't Be Concerned</u>

Daughter,

For months you have pondered the reasoning behind the excessive anger exhibited toward you from the one you least expected. I will now give you understanding. This anger is not aimed at you, but at me.

It was hoped that I would allow the continuation of the lies and deceit, but when I demanded a clean sweep, and decreed that truth and revelation was released, anger was the result. In that person's eyes, I am the blame for all of the troubles. I want you to know that I am dealing in this situation.

I have seen the misery, and the turmoil of your mind. I have seen the worrying and the wondering why these things have happened to you. You were placed close by for a short season, but now I must deal with the perpetrator. My help can only be sought by no other than this individual, and I require a broken and contrite spirit before I can extend my hand of deliverance.

Do not despise the time spent in this place, the enemy would tell you that it was all for nothing, but I assure you this night that I will get glory from the entire thing.

It is now time for you to step into a new pool of cool water that I have for you. This water will change you and it shall flow from deep within your spirit.

Do not concern yourself with what is going on around you, just know that I am working out what is best for your life.

Working in your behalf,
Father

Dear Working Father,

I thank you for giving to me understanding about the things that have caused me concern.

I am thankful for the love you have showed to me by revealing deceptive hidden things. Sometimes I think that I would have preferred to stay in ignorance about the situation, but you are a God of light, and you want me informed about the things going on around me.

You took me out of the darkness and the deception that had surrounded me and pulled me into the light.

I did not want to leave my comfortable place, the trickery kept me from seeing truth, and even now, it is difficult to grasp. I sound just like Israel wanting to go back to Egypt.. I am ashamed, thank you for delivering me.

Now that my eyes have adjusted to the light, I see more clearly.

Thank you for the healing and deliverance that is available to all of us through the name of Jesus.

I receive your fresh new touch upon my soul. I am healed and delivered by your powerful Spirit.

My life is in your hands, thank you for working everything out for my good.

I pray in Jesus' name,

Walking in light,
Your Refreshed Daughter

Psalms 108:1 Oh, God, my heart is fixed; I will sing and give praise to You with all my might.

Give Your All

Daughter,

Give your all into my hands. I do have a work for you to do for me. You have been wondering how much of your dreaming about the vision is real or simply imaginary. All of it is in my hands and I can bring every detail to fruition at my will.

Every dream I have caused you to believe in was given for the sole purpose of motivating you to stretch and believe for the seemingly impossible. I do not measure success by few or many. Every soul that is helped can not be calculated in value, I do not want one soul left behind.

In the case of the one you have prayed for so long, I have told you before, I am bringing back the prodigal to my side. Your willingness to help others has freed my hand to release and rescue. My child, will love me again and repent of the many years of avoiding my presence.

Prophecy is "forth telling," just wanted you to know ahead of time. My timing is perfect. Do not fear the words of those proclaiming they know what I am saying to you. If their words do not align themselves with my voice speaking to you, set them upon a shelf. Fear brings doubt and confusion. You must stand against these things.

There are those around you that have a tendency to lash out and wound. I have this thing on a leash, so far, and no more. Pray for wisdom that deliverance and healing will touch their lives.

There are those that concern themselves with thoughts of being responsible for you. Tell them you have someone who has promised to see to your every need.

Keep self-pity away from your door, for I will have pity upon you. You are not just anyone; you will be cared for in the manner I have chosen for you. I have planned out each life in detail, but each must follow the blue print I have made for them.

Some go their own way, missing my provisions. Do not waste any more time treading out the sour grapes, I have a vintage harvest awaiting you.

Father

Father,

I do give every thing in my life to you. The dreams you have planted in my heart are real, and they are alive with your power. Nothing is impossible, and every God given dream will come to pass.

Thank you for delivering my family, I confess in advance that they are sold-out followers of the Lord Jesus Christ, walking in his ways, serving him with joy and gladness.

In Jesus' name I resist fear of man. I hear your voice and a stranger's voice I will not follow. I stand against confusion and doubt.

Thank you that you have promised that you will never leave or forsake me, therefore, I can count on you to meet all of my needs because I am your child, having covenant rights promised long ago to Abraham.

Because of Jesus, the promises given to Abraham are mine. Blessing you will bless me, and multiplying you will multiply me. I receive the blessings of the covenant right now.

I do not allow self-pity to rob me of my blessings. I do not need pity from anyone but the Lord. Thank you for your plan for my life. It is the Lord's plan that I want in my life, and not my own.

Father, no more looking back at sour experiences of the past, I see fields of golden grain, and receive from that harvest field.

I pray in Jesus' name,

Your Grain-Gathering Daughter

Psalms 108:13   Through God we will have victory for He treads down the enemy.

My Purposes

Daughter,

I am telling you now that everything you are experiencing is for my purpose and plan. You cannot see as I do, but this plan will lead to days of heaven on earth for you. Rest your worried mind and trust in my unseen hand.

As you are waiting for my miracles, look at each day with a new mentality. See my plan unfolding right before your eyes, each day brings you closer to the fulfillment of your dreams.

Sometimes things seem so out of whack, but that is simply your perception of things. No one is winning here except me. I am the Almighty God of your help. I crush the enemy, there is none that can deny my presence and live.

I want you to begin seeing me as all that I am to you. I am first of all on your side. All doubts as to the outcome of the battle are settled. I fight for you, no contest!

Sometimes your mind struggles attempting to make my face look in your direction. I have never turned away from you. You have always had my attention.

Now let me work unhindered. I already know when and how your deliverance is coming. Relax and enter into faith, allow no more interference from the enemy of your soul.

I've got you covered!

Purposeful Father

Dear Purposeful Father,

Thank you, Father, that you have filtered all of the things in my life. Nothing is happening to me except that which will bring me to the place where my destiny is waiting. I receive the days of heaven on earth that you have promised.

My mind is at rest as I see your unseen hand guiding, guarding all the way. I see your hand with the eye of faith. Thank you for changing me so that now I approach each day with a new mentality. I look with amazement at the plan you are unfolding right before my eyes.

Each day I am increasingly aware that I am closer to the fulfillment of my dreams. When things seem out of sync, I am conscious of the fact that this is just my perception of things, and not yours. You are the only one winning the fight. The enemy always loses.

I thank you that you are the Almighty God of my help. Lord, I can't make it without your help. powerful is your name; your enemies are ground to powder, and fall at your feet.

Father, show me all that you are, and all that you want me to be. I am confident of one thing…. you are on my side, the battle results are in, and I win!

Your eyes are always upon me, Father. I have always been blessed by your gaze upon me. Thank you.

Knowing all of these things I now let go, and step out of your way. I allow your will and your plan to be performed. I am really enjoying the rest of God, I am in the faith zone and refuse to allow the enemy to speak to my mind or emotions.

Thank you for covering me completely.

I pray in Jesus' name,

Purposely Resting Daughter

Psalms 109:30-31   I will give loud praises to the Lord among many people for He stands at the right hand of the poor to save them.

I Looked After You

Daughter,

Have I not looked after your needs? Have I proved myself faithful? You have not fully understood that your prayers work miracles. I really do hear and answer when you call.

All of heaven knows your name, many are petitioning me on your behalf. You have blessed others, and now their prayers for your safety and well-being are reverberating throughout my halls of justice.

I am your advocate, your defense attorney. My scales of justice are now in my hand, and they have tipped in your favor. I have not found you wanting.

Remember the account in scripture when I informed the Persian King Balthazar that he had been weighed in the balance and had been found wanting. I am setting the scales aside and have risen to bring justice in your life.

In the dispensation of grace, you are acquitted, declared not guilty, because of the shed blood at Calvary. You are covered by Jesus' blood, and I now look upon you with mercy and love. All of your past sins and iniquities are put away, locked out of sight, never again to resurface and make a curtain call.

They are banished into the deepest sea of my forgetfulness. They are completely out of my sight, never to be remembered against you again.

Comfort one another with these words.

Redeeming my loved ones,
Father

Dear Redeeming Father,

You have blessed me with everything that I have needed, and even beyond. You always meet my need with abundance; you are faithful and true. It is beginning to sink in that my prayers are heard in Heaven, and that I always receive answers.

Father, I didn't realize that my name is known in Heaven. I am so thankful for the people of prayer that loved me enough to fall upon their knees and seek your help for me in this time of trouble. I bless your prayer warriors in the name of Jesus.

Your mercy endures forever; I praise you today for the kindness that you have extended to me. Thank you for arising and issuing the commands that release your help to me. Scripture tells me to leave all judgment calls to you, I have done this and now I thank you for bringing forth justice to me.

Thank you that I have you as my defense attorney. Thank you for the shed blood of the Lord Jesus Christ. This sacrifice now declares me not guilty of all sin. Every thing of shame and failure is now under the blood of Christ. No more encores or reminders of past sins, everything has been permanently removed by the Holy Spirit.

I receive your comfort in this knowledge.

In Jesus' name I pray,

Your Client Daughter

Psalms 110:1   The Lord said to me, sit at my right hand and I will make your enemies your footstool.

Hold on to Your Faith

Daughter of Faith,

Hold on to your faith; the enemy will not lie down and play dead. He is ever on the move, looking for a victim, but my security patrol, led by the Spirit of God, has you covered.

Fear nothing for I am a Mighty God, full of great power and my hand is upon you to bring about a great deliverance.

Wake up, cry no more...your deliverer is here. I have snapped your chains, and carried you out of the enemy's camp. I will now take you to my place for total restoration and healing. You will heal, and you will be resurrected and flow with me.

Much activity is coming into your life. You will become very busy for me. In your activities, do not forget me, for I am your source of life.

Your very life depends upon me. I pump your heart and tell it how many days it must function properly so you can do what I have commanded you to do.

I know you are feeling somewhat fatigued, but you will notice I will multiply your rest, and you will awaken and be refreshed by my Spirit.

Make way, I am preparing open doors of ministry, and your life will never again be the same. You will experience such excitement! The lame will walk, and the blind will see. Demons will flee as my anointing sweeps through the places where my Spirit will send you.

Let me lead the way. I will do all the work; you simply follow behind me. I will place you center stage, and there will be no effort on your part.

Multiplying you,
Father

Dear Multiplying Father,

According to your instructions, I am tightening my grip on my faith. I am thankful that you keep me protected from the enemy. Thank you for your hand upon me, and for the great deliverance I am receiving.

I receive your comfort and thank you for drying my tears. You are my deliverer, and my chains have been broken. Thank you for rescuing me, and for the total restoration you are bringing to me. I love being in your arms.

I look forward to our time together, thank you for using me in your ministry to people. I do not forget that I need you every moment of every day. Thank you for the multiplication of rest to me, I love your refreshing. Thank you for the open doors of ministry, I love being busy for you.

I love exciting days, thank you for the demonstration of your anointing as we walk together through these open doors. Thank you for doing it without any help from anyone. I am following you step by step.

Have your way in my life, I yield to your purpose and plan.

I pray in Jesus' name,

Thankfully,
Your Busy Daughter

Psalms 111:10 **The fear of the LORD is the beginning of wisdom. A good understanding have all they that do his commandments. Praise will be his forever.**

Hold Your Head High

Daughter,

Hold your head high, with no shame. Accept the assignment that I have for you, I have chosen you for my purposes.

I want you to realize things are going to start happening fast. You will be on the fast track in the things of God; that will be the order of the day.

No sooner will you walk through one door, and then another will open behind it. There is much to be done in the days ahead, and I will confound the wise of the land.

I have placed my sentinel by your bedside and he will stand guard about you. I have assigned additional angels to watch over your loved ones.

Expect my miracles; they are heading your way. Your new address is called "Miracle Way." I will bless and keep you.

My children really know what it is to be free. Celebrate your freedom from the chains of hell that once held you captive. Revelation is beginning to flow. Your heart has been opened wide to receive my power and my glory. It shall flow fresh from my Holy Mountain.

The Holy Spirit power you received so many years ago can be matched, doubled, and quadrupled for I have fresh fire that will burn off warrior fatigue. Stay fresh, alive with my Spirit, and I will do exploits through your hands.

Supporting you,
Father

Dear Supportive Father,

I thank you for removing my shame, and for being the one that lifts my head.

I bow myself before you and humbly receive your assignment. I will do what you ask of me.

Thank you for strengthening me as the doors begin to open and my life becomes busy doing your work. Thank you for your angel that guards me. Thank you that he has been instructed to watch over my loved ones as well.

I expect your miracles. I love miracles! This new address is something to shout about.

I celebrate the freedom you have given me, no more chains. Thank you for revelation knowledge, I receive it with thanksgiving in my heart.

I receive all of the additional power of the Holy Spirit that you have for me. Your Spirit has burned away my warrior fatigue.

Thank you that I am alive and fresh with your touch.

In Jesus' name I pray,

Devotedly,
Your Miracle Daughter

Psalms 113:5   Who is like the LORD, our God who lives on high?

Battle Cry!

Daughter,

I am calling my leaders from one area of ministry to another. I am requiring my leaders to line up and report for duty.

New orders are being issued; for I have need of my generals, and I am repositioning them into new fields of service.

Some are bewildered and perplexed by these sudden changes but tell them when they ask, "the Lord has need of you!"

Your Father

Dear Father,

My ears are open to your call, for you have said that you have need of me.

Everywhere you send me I will tell others about Jesus, and the love of God that is demonstrated through his life.

I will take your light into the darkness, bringing life, love, and hope, to a hurting world.

Obediently,
Your Daughter

Psalms 114:7   Earth, tremble at the presence of the Lord!

Upcoming Events

Daughter,

Let me speak to you about upcoming events. Come closer that you may hear my voice.

Slow your pace, still your mind, and my voice will be heard.
I am gathering those I wish you to minister to. I will speak incredible information in your ears.

It is late, rest now, but be expecting! These events are just around the corner.

Many attitudes from your family will be adjusted; I love you my little one, and desire peace and tranquility to reside in your family.

Omnipresent Father

Dear Omnipresent Father,

My ears are open to listen to the things you want to discuss with me.

I have quieted my mind, slowed down my busy schedule, and have turned aside to sit at your feet. I put away my Martha apron, and have become a Mary. I receive your Words to me today.

It is incredible enough that you would love me and wish to have fellowship with me, but to hear you say that you will share your secrets is joy to the max!

I thank you for the suddenly blessings. My family is blessed by your love. Thank you Lord. Thank you for your love, peace, and tranquility in my family.

Expectantly,
Your Quieted Daughter

Psalms 116:1   I love the LORD, because he has heard my voice and my prayers.

Sparkle Time

Daughter,

I am giving you time to rest and heal, and I am continually watching your progress.

Sometimes it doesn't appear that I am paying close attention. This is not the case. If I had not intervened for you, there would have been an escalation of the tearing and wounding. I will only allow so much and then judgment comes. I look after my own.

We have much to do before your work on earth is completed. I do not expect you to make things happen, if fact, I would rather you didn't.

Each person has his or her own distinctive call from me. I want you to flow along with me, I love seeing you flow in my Spirit. I love anointing you, and watching you sparkle under that anointing. We have a great time together, don't we!

I am going to open more doors for you than ever before. Others will not understand how this is so. They will question both of us as to how all of this happened.

The open doors will be to places where your gifting will be respected, and where you will receive just compensation as a worker worthy of her hire. The crowds will be touched by my precious, powerful, anointing and will desire to see it go forth and touch a lost and dying world.

Sickness is a curse and I will touch lives through your obedience to my call.

The enemy thought his most recent attack would ruin you for good. He still doesn't know what I am going to do for you. Wait until you see what I am going to do. You are going to be so happy, I promise you, and it will not be a long period of time in coming.

Get ready, get ready, and get ready! It is time to be blessed. Bind these words to your heart; let them be a reality to you, sinking down deep within.

From Father

Dear Father,

Thank you for the wisdom you give me as I rest and heal. Your eye is always observing my progress.

I may not see your attention in the matters that concern my soul, but I know your ways and I know that you are ever present working on these things.

Thank you for rescuing my life. I thank you for taking care of your child. I am unique to you Lord, you are not a cookie cutter creator, and each person is especially made for your pleasure.

Just call me 'Sparkle," for I intend to shine for the whole world to see. I will get on fire with your Spirit and the whole world will come just to see me burn!

Thank you for open doors to share your good news. I also thank you for providing the necessary funds for the growth of the ministry. I yield to you to be used to touch a lost and dying world. Thank you for your healing anointing.

None of the enemy's attacks have hit their target, thank you for your patriot missile system that takes him out in a flash.

Regardless of attacks, your plan moves forward in my life. I love being happy, and I receive your Word to me that I will indeed experience joy and happiness beyond comparison to what I've had before. Thank you that this will be done speedily.

I embrace your Words to my heart, they are sinking deep within me now.

I pray in Jesus' name,

Your Ready Daughter

Psalms 119:105   Your word is a lamp for my feet and a light for my path.

Let's Talk

Daughter,

I like it that you desire to converse with me on a regular basis. Many blessings are lining up and heading your way because of this. The prayers of your friends and family, combined with your faith, have set the stage and are a backdrop for your miracles.

Become accustomed to miracles, believe for miracles, and sow seed for miracles. Be at ease living in this realm, because this is what I can do for you with no effort at all! Miracles are easy for me.

Welcome my presence into your life, I will reach out to the world through your hands.

Finances placed within your hands can easily be multiplied again and again. The enemy's power to harass you about finances has been broken. Now you will begin to flow in prosperity. Use wisdom, let me show you where to place your money.

I am now increasing your sensitivity to my Spirit. You are listening more attentively to my counsel.

Prayers for your safety and well-being have reached my throne, and I have risen to defend you. When I stand to defend you, nothing can get in my way, and no one can change my mind.

My power is so much greater than your mind can entertain.

Lovingly,
Omnipotent Father

Dear Omnipotent Father,

I thank you for allowing me these times to share my heart with you. I now understand that time in your presence brings blessings my way. You are so giving and kind.

I thank you that everything is now ready for my miracles to make their entrance. I desire to live in the realm of miracles, I want to be accustomed to your miracles.

I invite your presence into my life, and as I do this, you will use me to change the lives or others.

Thank you for financial increase. I receive your increase beginning today. The devil's hold over my money is broken in Jesus' name. I now receive your wisdom and direction in handling finances.

Thank you for your defense system. I believe it is better than any defense system that this world has ever seen.

Your power is truly amazing; nothing can withstand you. Thank you for your power.

In Jesus' name I pray,

Obediently,
Your Miracle Daughter

Psalms 120: 1   In my distress I cried out to You LORD, and you heard me.

Impatience

Beloved Daughter,

Impatience tries to cover you like a garment. I am working to bring a healing in this area of your life. My Spirit is bringing you to a place where the outcome of this battle is simply this... a victory for you!
You will receive it with gladness, but keep your focus on the other meaningful things that each day brings.

Not all things that are being taught are based upon the authority of my Word. Everything you teach must line up with my Word. Stressful pressing, and intense battling are not always required. I am your warrior ,and you are my beloved.

Spend time getting to know your husband, for you are my bride. Allow my presence to comfort and console you. Enjoy the days set before you.

I know it all. Ask for my details and I will give them to you. I have a life for you where my thoughts will be yours. Seek me with your whole heart, for it is then that you will see my manifested presence.

Receive of me now, and I will impart my rest to you.

Blessings from Father

Dear Blessing Father,

Father by your grace and help, I am now shedding the garment of impatience. Thank you for your help and healing of this weakness.

Thank you for the victory in my battles, I receive your victories with gladness in my heart. I will not forget to look upon the many blessings you give each day.

My desire is to know your Word, I ask that your Spirit keep me bulls eye center in the Word of God, I'll not climb out on any limbs featuring off- centered teachings.

I love being your bride, the object of your affection. I embrace your love and comforting presence in my life. I enjoy our times together.

My bags are packed, and I am ready to travel with you. I am thankful that you love to fill in all of the blanks.

Thank you for the privilege of hearing your thoughts about situations surrounding me.

I desire to see you in your fullness, and I now seek you with my whole heart.

Thank you for your promised rest, I receive all of your promises to me.

I pray in Jesus' name,

Obediently,
Your Patient Daughter

> **Psalms 121:1-2   I will lift up my eyes to the hills. Where does my help come from? It comes from the LORD who made heaven and earth.**

Never Too Late

Daughter,

Keep reminding yourself that life is simply a journey. On a journey, many things are experienced; some good and some not so good. Rejoice in the fact that I never leave nor abandon my people. You have supernatural help, and this help makes the difference in your life.

Know that it is never too late to prosper. I hold you in my hand...total care and control. I am about to spring you from your cocoon. Look for good things to happen, not bad.

I am able to straighten the cockeyed things in your life. Give me some time. I am working on things that involve your life. I will place loved ones back beside you, have no worry about that. I know the future as well as the past. Put your hand in my hand now, and be like a trusting child. I will stay with you and help you.

The harvest fields are bulging with fruit. I will bless you for your obedience. It makes no difference if all turn their back on you and flee. I will never leave you alone. Haven't I proved that to you even in the house where you now reside?

Things do come to an end. Trust me to guide you into a new place in me. This season and this work I have been doing in you is drawing to a close.

Welcome with hope, and faith, the new that is coming. Don't allow your enemy to push. I am powerful enough to place you in an appropriate place.

Trust my unseen hand. Bow down and worship me because I miss our times together.

Father

Dear Father,

I thank you that my life is an exciting, wonderful journey that you have given to me as a gift. From this day forth, I will be thankful for life, and with your help, I will enjoy the journey. In times when I feel alone, I will remind myself that you have promised never to leave or forsake me.

Wow, I have a Father who is supernatural, able to do anything he wishes to do! I place myself in your hand and my life is certain to change for the better. The promise to take total care and control of the events in my life brings me comfort.

Thank you for changing me, I remember the time when I was a real mess, but now those days are behind me. The changes you have made have enriched my life beyond anything I could have imagined.

Thank you for restoring my life. My life is in yours now, and I will be your trusting child. Father, my heart is comforted knowing that you will never abandon me; you stay closer than any one I've ever counted on.

Father, I will obey your call, your sickle is in my hand, and I'm heading to the harvest fields. I welcome all of the new things you intend to bring into my life, thank you for providing everything I have need of.

My heart is bowed before you now; I worship you for you are worthy.

I've missed you too, Lord. I'm back where I belong.

In Jesus' name I pray,

Your Field Worker Daughter

> **Psalms125:   They that trust in the LORD will be like a strong mountain that cannot be removed, but remains forever.**

Rest, Forget About Yesterday

Daughter,

Let the past be the past. I will show you what to retain and what to let go. The enemy doesn't have nearly the power that some attribute to him.

I separate and remove troublesome encounters, yesterday is gone forever; and today you need my Spirit's love and guidance. Fear not that I will leave you behind. My Spirit is within you, marking you one of my own.

I have placed within you a great mantle of my presence. My power and anointing rests upon you.

Rest awhile,
Father

Rest-Giving Father,

I thank you for the wisdom to know what to keep, and what to throw away. Some things I thought I needed. You knew better.

Thank you for stepping in and removing anything that is harmful in my life. I am thankful for the Holy Spirit's love and guidance. He is within my spirit, leading, guiding, and guarding all the way.

I refuse to give the Devil credit for anything. You are my Warrior King! Your spirit within me is your seal, the down payment on all that you have promised. You will never leave or forsake me.

Thank you for the great mantle of your presence, your power and anointing resting upon me is too precious for words.

In Jesus' name I pray,

Your Sealed Daughter

Psalms 127:1   Only if the LORD builds a house, will it stand. The builders will be working in vain.

A Better Way

Daughter,

Life doesn't have to be sad and lonely. I will show you a better way.

I see the future as well as the past, and I say to you, "sunshine is just ahead of you!" The enemy tries working to produce stress and worry. Has anything he has threatened materialized? He is just a braggart, threatening much, but delivering little.

He knows where to attack you, and challenges you often in that area. Often, it is in the area of your self-esteem. You are very special to me. Do not think too little of yourself. I am working out a plan for you; trust in my unseen hand. When things surface from your unhealed areas, just know that I have turned up the heat, and the impurities have risen to the top. This is good, for then I will remove the impurities, and healing will spring forth.

Do not back down from your adversary; he has to move, not you. My power and anointing is in you and I will direct it to change your own life.

Stand against doubt and unbelief. All things are possible to them that believe! Be a believing believer, one that will challenge the impossible in your life. I desire to do a new thing in you.

Humility is being woven into the fabric of your being. This had to be accomplished before I could manifest this new thing. This work is nearly complete, and we are now ready to move forward, leaving the old, and embracing the new.

Waste no more time on what could have been. My goodness lies before you in your future. Leave the old tattered garments in the dust, and let us now go to the wardrobe room and see what compliments you now. I want a garment on you that becomes the station in life where you are now standing.

Know that the battle is raging. Saints throughout the world are in battle. My word promises that I will cause you to triumph. The battle is mine! Remind yourself of this. The enemy is no match for me; allow me to fight for you. Were you serious when you said you would go for me? Will you go even thought the way is often difficult?

Tell me what you need, and see if I will not meet that need in abundance.

Faithful is My Name

Dear Faithful Father,

I thank you for the sunshine highway ahead. This is a much better road than I've previously traveled. My future is bright and joyful in you. In Jesus' name, I rebuke all stress and worry.

Nothing the enemy says will come to pass because he is a liar and the father of every lie. I command his hands tied in Jesus' name, no more threats. In Jesus' name, I will not back down to the adversary, I will not move but he will. I refuse all doubt and unbelief, for with God all things are possible.

I thank you for healing any low self-esteem in my mind. I have allowed others to speak into my life as to their perception of me, but no more! I am special to the Lord Jesus and He sees value in me.

Thank you for the plan that you have for my life, I thank you that it is a plan for my good, and not for evil. You plan to prosper me and give me hope and a future. Thank you Lord for the fire that causes all of the impurities of my heart to be removed by your Spirit.

I am a believing believer, and in the name of Jesus I challenge the impossible things in my life. I humble myself in the sight of the Lord, and now I am leaving the ways of the past, and walking into the destiny God has for me.

All of the old has been dropped to the ground. I am shopping in the Lord's wardrobe palace, and have found the clothing he has designed especially for me.

Thank you for always causing me to triumph, In you, I am a serious contender.

Father, you lead, and I will follow.

In Jesus' name I pray,

Your Humble Daughter

> **Psalms 136:23   God remembered us when we were in our sorrows; for his mercy endures forever.**

Blessings Continue

Daughter,

My blessings will continue upon you because you have a heart after me and have a love for my people. Let me bless you. Fear not, for I am with you to bless your life.

Allow the flow to come your way. I am different than any earthly father. Welcome me into your life. During times of pressure, just sing "I cast all of my cares upon you, I lay all of my burdens down at your feet,". As your faith reaches out to me, I will begin to move mountains for you. As my blessings begin to pour into your life you will sing a song of victory.

Sometimes the enemy finds an area of weakness, he attempts to move in close so he can torment and harass. He knows what weapon works with every individual. In your case, he has been working using fear and lack of trust to knock you to the ground.

Allow my Spirit to have complete control. I will show you where to go and it will be the best place for you, and your trust in me will grow.

My judgment is impeccable; never question my decisions because my eye is keen, missing nothing. There are reasons why you have had to walk certain paths. In the days to come the reasons will become crystal clear.

Learn all you can during this quiet time. I am ready to move you into what will benefit my Kingdom. There are people all around you that have needs. Minister to those I send to you.

Father

Dear Father Who Keeps Blessing Me,

My heart is touched every day by your love for me. Thank you for these blessings. I have tossed fear out the back door, and now I am determined that I will trust in your love. Your love is not conditional.

The Word says that you are love, and that you loved me while I was still in my sins. Awesome! Thank you for the songs you give me to sing; the adversary hates to hear me sing. I will lift my voice in praise to you for the things you have brought me through.

Father, I thank you for restoring my trust and healing my fears. Now I can walk forward into the good things that you have for me. I trust your judgment; your eye sees everything, and your ear is privy to conversations spoken behind my back. I surrender full control to the Holy Spirit. He knows where you want me, and the best place for my life.

It is my desire to learn from you, teach me I pray. I will love and care for those that cross my path, and this will benefit your Kingdom.

In Jesus' name I pray,

Your Song Bird Daughter

Psalms 138:8   The LORD will perfect that which concerns me. O LORD, your mercy endures forever. Remember me, LORD, for I am your creation, your child.

Believe

Daughter,

You have known about believing and receiving and at times have attempted to walk in this, there were times that you have lacked the perseverance to stay with it. As a result you have failed to receive some prayer answers that were needed.

Be steady in believing, knowing I am on your side. You are not fighting and wrestling me, attempting to twist my arm. You have an enemy that is a thief, and he will take from you anytime he can.

The battles are often fierce. You have heard, "no pain, no gain." Some things are worth fighting for. Keep your priorities in the right place; watch your words and your believing. You will gain much as you do this.

Praying in the Holy Spirit aids you immensely. Trust me; I love you and want you to heed my counsel.

The answer to this believing and receiving is patience. The world says, "Rome wasn't built in a day." Think about that. You didn't get where you are now on an overnight trip. Give me some time to turn things around. Some things I will turn suddenly, some turn more slowly, but surely.

I have angels to spare to take care of the needs of all my children.

So many times my people are nearly to their breakthrough and give up prematurely.

A premature birth brings miscarriage and loss. Let me encourage you today because I have many good things I wish to do for you. Reach out in faith, the God kind of faith.

Have the joy of knowing a prayer answering God!

My child, move ahead in faith, knowing I care for you and wish to watch over and help with every detail of your life. A loving, caring Father is what I am to you! The effects of having an earthly father who neglected giving you affection has caused you problems in relating to me. It is something that battles you still.

Your True Father

Dear True Father,

I now see more clearly that it is the determined one wanting to finish the race that receives the prize. Forgive me for the times I set down and gave up. No more lost promises for me, I am determined now to stand for the duration. With your help I will stand until you hand to me my victory crown.

Thank you for sitting on my side of the arena, your last training sessions brought me to a place of success.

Lord, I am guarding every word that is leaving my mouth; I've heard that loose lips sink ships!

You tell me that I will have the things that I say, so nothing but faith filled words will roll off my tongue.

Thank you for the Holy Spirit who prays through me, he prays a perfect prayer and I thank you for that. I thank you for suddenlies, but if it takes time to turn situations around, I will stand and believe you will do it.

Thank you for the ministry of your angels. Your Word says that they minister to the heirs of salvation; I'm one of your heirs, so I am happy they work for me.

I will not abort the dreams you have caused me to believe in, no miscarriages, and loss will I allow. I reach out in faith today, having the God kind of faith, speaking those things that be not as though they were. Thank you that you are a prayer-answering Father. I receive your love and care over my life and thank you for helping with every thing that concerns me.

Thank you that you have enough affection to share with the entire world, I receive my portion now. Thank you for the good that was in my earthly father.

In Jesus' name I pray,

Your Full Term Daughter

Psalms 139:1-6   Lord, You have searched me and know me. You know when I sit and when I stand. You understand my hidden thoughts. You surround me when I am moving and when I am lying down. You alone are acquainted with all my ways. You know every word of my mouth. You know my past and my future. It is too wonderful for me to understand.

Set Your Sights

Daughter,

Set your sights upon the prize. A crown is awaiting you for being one who ran their race and won!

Whether you believe my words of comfort to you or choose to not believe, will make all the difference in how successful you navigate these waters.

Lean on me and I will see that you arrive in style!

Constant Father

Dear Constant Father,

My eyes are upon you Lord for you are my prize. Father, I thank you for the ability to complete the race that is set before me.

I know the enemy hates anyone that follows you, but in Jesus' name, I will follow you regardless of the difficulties that may arise. You, in me, are greater than the enemy out there, so onward I go.

I believe your Words to me, and your navigational charts will be followed, and cause my way to flow with great ease.

My heart is to know you, teach me your ways so that I may arrive in style.

In Jesus' name I pray,

Your Styling Daughter

Psalms 135:3   **The LORD who made heaven and earth, bless you.**

One Word

Daughter,

Remember that just one word from my lips can change your entire outlook on life. I have given you something to hope for, and it will not be taken away from you.

Today I speak words to you from the song, "Zion is calling me to a higher place of praise." I have told you again and again that I desire and intend to lift you up in ministry. Allow the freedom of the Spirit's power to indwell you.

Reach out to the multitudes of hurting mankind. I desire a vessel that I can flow through, and I am getting the job done through an unlikely source. Many will be surprised when I take you by the hand and raise you up. The unlikely candidate is not unlikely to me, I knew what I would do in you from the very beginning.

My angels hovered over you to protect and keep you. The battles over your well-being have been fierce, long, and tiring, but I the Lord your God will bring great rest to your soul and you will experience the peace of God in a supernatural way.

You are now at the mouth of the river getting ready to swim into the rich comforting water of my Spirit. I will reveal myself to you there. You have fought hard to get to this place. I have seen the times you have set yourself aside unto me, it was time well spent, now I will reward you openly.

I know your gifting must have an outlet, and that is what I will give to you. I will give you a place to minister my love and power. Don't argue with me about your inadequacies, I have given you everything that you need.

When the door opens, go through it. I will be going before you preparing the way. Recently I have removed individuals from your life, this had to be done to get you to this place. Now you see my faithfulness and their deceptions. You are to walk in love toward others, but not depend upon them to be what only I can be to you.

You need me; I am your rock and your friend. This is something you have found to be true. I didn't abandon you; didn't leave you to fend for yourself, but I came along and picked you up, and carried you to higher ground. I am your best friend.

Close to you,
Father

Dear Close Father,

I thank you for every Word that proceeds from your mouth to my ears. Nothing that you have spoken can be stolen from me. I thank you, Father, for this higher place of praise where you have lifted me... again. I yield to your Spirit and I desire to fulfill the call that is upon my life.

I thank you that you look at my heart, and not the mistakes of my past. Man would probably pass me by, but you have chosen me to represent you.

Your angels are ever-present with me; I sense them hovering close beside me all of the way. Thank you for the rest and peace that you have promised. It is exciting to know that I have reached a place where I will find what my soul has yearned for, I long to hear your voice giving revelation knowledge to me.

Thank you for open doors to share the gospel. I will no longer look at the imperfections and weaknesses of my life, but I will lift my eyes and see you in your perfection and power.

You do supply everything that I need. Thank you for loving me so much that you want me safe and protected by your Spirit. I trust your judgment regarding those I should walk with through this journey called life. Father, I ask that you choose my friends and acquaintances.

Father, I want your plan and your way. You are my rock and my best friend. Thank you for staying close by my side, never abandoning me to the evil wolves, lions, and bears.

I am now sitting high and secure out of the reach of all of my enemies.

In Jesus' name I pray,

Your Comforted Daughter

> **Psalms 135:4   For the LORD has chosen Jacob (me) unto himself; and Israel (me) for his peculiar treasure.**

Relax

Daughter,

Take a deep breath and relax in my presence. Your spirit is sensing a breakthrough on the horizon and is becoming anxious. I just want you to rest and enjoy your life; let me bring to you the things that I have promised. Struggling will not make things happen any sooner.

You cannot see the complexities of the things needing completion. I am working, angels are working, for I am remaining steadfast in my commitment to you.

Those who abandoned you, robbed you of your emotions and your possessions, have gone. Refuse to allow them to continue reaching into your life, and taking what is left.

The things that have been retained, lift up to me, and I will send reimbursement. The enemy is a thief, but my spirit has caught him. I have stopped his pilfering in your life.

He stands around the perimeter of your property and shouts his abuse. Because he has been removed, he now tries harassing from a distance, aiming his missiles at your mind.

Daily cover your mind with my thoughts and Words to you, release my angels to do battle against these poachers, they won't stay around long.

The enemy knows your ways of thinking, and he tries to plant seeds of discouragement into your thoughts. He is aware that he cannot stop what I am going to do for you, but he will attempt to make your journey as miserable as possible.

I am sovereign and each of your days are in my hand. Whatever they bring I have ordained. Bad things do happen in the lives of my people, but most of it can be avoided by listening and obeying my words of warning.

Regardless of present or future encounters with troubles, I am the one with the power to smash your enemies to powder.

Father

Dear Faithful Father,

Today I take a deep breath and relax in your presence. My breakthrough is on the horizon and I am excited to see the miracles that are heading in my direction.

Because of what you have done for me, I am entering into a place where I enjoy the wonders of each day. No more struggling now for I am at rest. Thank you for the work you are doing in me, I appreciate everyone involved with my deliverance.

In Jesus' name, I refuse to allow any additional thievery from the enemy. I now give everything into your hands, and I receive back everything that has been stolen.

Father, I thank you that even if missiles from the enemy are launched against me, your anti-missile defensive system is in full readiness to protect and keep me. I cover my mind on a daily basis with the Word of God, and remember you have given to me a security detail that stands guard 24-7. Thank you for your Angels.

My trust is in the name of the Lord. Your plan for my life is moving along according to schedule. The water under my feet is solid as a rock!

Thank you for your love and your power. You are sovereign, and everything you decree is absolutely perfect.

In Jesus' name I pray,

Your Safe Daughter

Psalms 135:9   Who sent signs and wonders into the middle of Egypt?

<u>Prayer-Answering God</u>

Daughter,

Do you not think that I am a prayer answering God? Many prayers have arisen in your behalf and I am bound by my Word to answer those cries of help for you.

Just because sometimes my wheels of justice move slowly, doesn't mean they aren't moving at all. It is not what you see or feel that matters; it is what I am doing! The Holy Spirit will constantly tell you what He is hearing from the Father and the Son.

The enemy loves planting his vision in your thoughts, but people of faith listen only to me. I am bringing revelation to you about why you are where you are in life right now.

The tremendous need to feel love and comfort was used as a weapon against you, but I am healing you as you step into my presence.

I haven't forgotten where you are, or what you need. Just because I have been silent about your destination, doesn't mean I will always be silent. I will show you the way at my proper time. You must hold on to me and I will provide and show you the way you are to go.

You can't give up after traveling this far with me. Soon your journey will be over and my comfort will be yours eternally. I have received much honor and glory from your life.

You have been a source of inspiration and hope to many. Your life has counted with me. Trust me for the remainder of the journey, I will give you rest...I will give you the answers that you seek.

Do you think it is a natural thing that friends are giving gifts to you during this time? They are praying people; they hear me and obey. I am trying to get your attention that I can and I will take care of you.

I need you in my fields. I will correct, fix, and heal all your wounds and troubles so that you can minister effectively. I will not demand you go unhealed. I want you well and happy. I will lead you gently and tenderly. I do not push or demand.

Prayer-Answering God

Dear Prayer-Answering Father,

I thank you that you are a prayer answering God. Your Word says that if we ask, we will receive. Many have prayed for breakthroughs for me and I know you have heard and will answer their prayers. I know you are working a work of patience in me. Regardless of how long it takes, I know your Spirit is resolving the problems now facing me.

I hear your voice and a stranger's voice I will not follow. I am a woman of faith, and hear what you are saying. Thank you for your hand upon my life. You have a plan to bless me, and show the direction my life should take.

I will not give up. You have been faithful to me in the past, and I have no reason to believe that you will leave me now. I trust you with my life, and I know that the answers I need, you will supply.

Thank you for moving upon the hearts of people to help me in this season of my life. I thank you for praying men and women of God that hear and obey.

I yield myself to your hand, Father. Touch, heal, and repair the areas that would hinder the call of God upon my life. Thank you for your gentle touch. I gratefully obey the leading of the Holy Spirit.

In Jesus' name I pray,

Your Fixable Daughter

Psalms 136:1-9 Oh, give thanks to the Lord, for he is good; for his mercy endures forever. He, alone, does great wonders. His wisdom made the heavens. He stretched out the earth. He made the sun, moon, and stars. His mercy endures forever.

Enjoy!

Dear Daughter,

Simply enjoy the day set before you. This continual pressing wears upon you. Relax, take things as they come; always standing in my power and authority.

I have been showing you the fickleness of human nature. With me, they shouted and praised me one day, but turned violent the next. People have not changed. True human nature will surface given the right circumstances.

The same ones, who swing away from you, can just as easily swing right back where they were. It depends upon what they can get from you at the time. I am not pleased when people try to use you for their purposes. I have purposes in mind for you, and if allowed, will bring those purposes to light.

You are my chosen vessel, not just any vessel, but one created for a divine purpose. Many of your battles were because of this chosen destiny.

Now is the season for great things to begin to happen, Let me have complete control, and I will make your life grand and your latter years will indeed be blessed beyond anything you have asked me for.

Let me do this my way. I have a carefully detailed plan. Let me unfold my plan. Listen intently for the call of my Spirit. There are many things you can do for me. Sort through those things and see which of them I will bless.

Don't be afraid of failure. My going to the cross, looked like a colossal failure. But victory was hidden in the failure. I will bring victory from every failed thing of your life.

Kick off the discouragement, dust off your dreams and begin to dream again of the good things I have for you.

Change is in the air, let the breeze carry you to your place called "there" It is time for me to strengthen and establish your life. Give me your hand . . . Stop looking at things with a negative view. I have many ministries inside of you. Don't despise your life. You keep looking at what you haven't done, and stop comparing yourself to others. You are made exactly to my specifications!

I am doing a tune-up on your emotions, major changes are in the works.

Father

Dear Heavenly Father,

I thank you for this day; I've made up my mind that I am going to enjoy each and every moment. I will stand in the authority you have given to me and I will use it each moment of the day.

Help me to see things as you do. Keep me safe from those that would yield themselves to the flesh and the devil. I trust you to place the people in my life that you desire, and removing those that are planted by the enemy of my soul.

Thank you for choosing me to be a vessel for you. Pour your Spirit on me, and allow me to pour out to the thirsty travelers I meet. Thank you for this new season, one in which your blessings will really begin to flow.

I yield to the direction of the Holy Spirit, asking that you show me your plan for my life. My ways have led to trouble, so no more of that. My ears are open to your instructions.

I rebuke fear of failure in Jesus' name, and claim victory even from the past failures of my life.

I believe you will bring good from every attempt I have made to serve you. My dreams have been pulled from the shelf and dusted off, and I am daring to dream again. You are my dream giver.

I receive your Spirit to carry me to the place where I need to be. Here's my hand, thank you for holding it the remainder of the journey. No more negativity. I choose to see what you see in me. I receive the ministry call you have placed upon me, and I totally yield to it right now in Jesus' name.

I will no longer compare myself to others; you have made me unique and special to accomplish your purpose upon this earth. Thank you for the maintenance work on my emotions, I have needed your touch.

In Jesus' name I pray,

Your Chosen Vessel

Psalms 136:1, 10-16   Oh, give thanks to the Lord, for he is good; for his mercy endures forever. He brought his children from captivity, he parted the sea; he led his children through the wilderness

Confessions of Your Mouth

Daughter,

The confession of your mouth can begin to turn the course of your life around quickly. Words are powerful, especially words the Holy Spirit has breathed upon. Words like: "God is turning my life around today!" or "my life is getting more exciting and happier with every breath I take!" or "God Almighty is in charge of my life!"

I have taught you what not to say, so now begin speaking what I am, and all that I am doing and will do for you.

Once your life on earth is over, none of this, the things of the past, will matter. All will seem as nothing. In the meantime, do you not think I can give you a wonderful, happy life now? Don't settle for mere existence, but reach for a higher plain.

I have seen the trickery of the devil plotting against your life. The things you can't change simply turn over to me. If I feel restoration of that particular situation need resurrected, then I shall see that it is done.

Regardless of the outcome, my hand is holding you.

Father

Dear Father,

I thank you for teaching me to guard the words of my mouth.

I ask the Holy Spirit to anoint my words so I will only speak words that will bless the hearers. Your Spirit places a guard upon my mouth keeping idle words, those non-productive, lack of faith, trash talk words, to remain silent at your command.

Thank you that one day, I will rejoice that I said yes to your call, and everything that troubled me on this journey will be as nothing.

Yes, you can and will, give to me a happy blessed life, Jesus promised it to me and he cannot lie. I receive your blessings today.

I will not settle for mere existence, but expect a life that has been promised to me by my Savior.

Father, I thank you that your eye doesn't miss a thing. You will take care of everything that concerns me and anything that needs corrected, you will correct.

I turn over to you every single problem and care that I have, and I thank you for carrying my load. I know your hand rests upon me now and forever.

In Jesus' name I pray,

Your Word-Speaking Daughter

Psalms 136:26   Oh, give thanks unto the God of Heaven for His mercy endures forever.

You Have My Attention

Daughter,

The enemy has fought hard to keep you from the place where you now stand. Brace yourself for battle, you stand, and I will fight for you!

Your mind tries getting in the fight, make it be still, I am your warrior and your victory, and the battle is mine.

Let go, and don't allow memories of past things shape your today. The enemy is throwing everything he has at you to get you to doubt me. He knows you will remain motionless in that state. You have more going for you than you think.

There are others, young and old, in this world that has suffered loss, humiliation, rejection, and financial reverses. Most do not know my power, and how hard it is for them.

You are familiar with my ways. You have been taught by me to fight and win. Put this knowledge into practice and begin to see the tide of the battle turn. Commands things to line up with my Word.

You will then smell the "Sweet Smell of your Success!"

Your situation, age, or abilities do not limit me. I have no limits and if you will trust me, I will take all of the hurts away and give you a brand new start. You do not need to fight to get my attention or favor, it is yours now. Walk in it!

Father

Dear Father,

I thank you that regardless of my opponent's tactics, I am now standing strong in the place where I belong. In Jesus' name I am braced for whatever he dishes out, because you do all of the fighting for me and you are a mighty warrior. I stand strong upon the Word of God, and believe for great victories.

I have ordered my mind to the corner of the arena, and I have commanded it to be still and silenced. You do not need any help in gaining victory for me, thank you Lord.

In Jesus' name I will not doubt you, or your ability to bring victory to my life. The devil is a liar, and I will not listen to him. Father, I pray for people all over the world that are suffering loss and pain. Raise up a wall of protection for them right now in Jesus' name.

Thank you for teaching me your ways, I now put this knowledge into practice in the daily situations of life, and I know that I will see the tide of the battle turn in my favor.

In Jesus' name, I command that the thief's hands are tied, I command things to line up with God's Word, and I now receive the sweet success that God has promised.

I thank you that you are limitless. There is no lack with you.

Thank you for the promise of a fresh new start, I thank you that your mercies are new every morning. Your attention to my care is wonderfully appreciated.

Thank you for the favor bestowed upon me. I walk in all that you have spoken to me.

In Jesus' name I pray,

Your Successful Daughter

Psalms 138:6-7   Though the LORD is high, he respects the lowly. Even when I am in the middle of trouble, He revives me and his hand saves me.

Dread

Daughter,

At times, you have a fear of suffering loss once again. I have said to you that regardless of the number of times you have suffered loss; I can still give back and fill your life again. Trust me my daughter.

I will bring you through this period of your life, and the losses will be regained. Happiness is what I want for you and I know just how to achieve that end.

Remember you are conversing with an on-time God! Watch me work in your behalf. I can give you more than you had before. Rejoice in that knowledge.

My eye saw these present happenings long before they were formed, nothing escapes my glance. I have provided a way of escape, there is one, and you will find it.

Sometimes, finding your way is like a checkerboard experience, you jump from one square, to another, to yet another. Never fear change, a better way can be in that change. Search your heart, the answer will be there.

Father

Dear Father,

I thank you that you are always faithful to keep me in your care. My trust is in your unchanging love and faithfulness.

Thank you in advance for returning everything that I have lost. I am thankful that you are on my side, always wanting the very best for me.

I know that you see every moment of my life and have made provisions for my good. Thank you for the way of escape, you have said that you have provided a way of escape and that I will find it. That is good news to me. I bless your name.

I will no longer fear change, you have my moves planned ahead of time, and I will follow your rules of the game and win overwhelmingly!

Father, search my heart, and as I walk before you I will look within my heart as well. As you reveal areas needing correction, I will yield to your revelation.

In Jesus' name I pray,

Your Obedient Daughter

> **Psalms 139:7-14** **Where could I go to be away from you?**
> **How could I ever be out of your presence? If I went to heaven,**
> **you would be there and if I were in hell, You would be there.**
> **If I took the wings of the morning and went to the farthest part**
> **of the sea, you would be there, and your hand would hold me.**
> **Even in darkness, you are a light for me. For you own even**
> **my inward parts from before my birth. I will praise You, Lord,**
> **for I am fearfully and wonderfully made. Your creativity is**
> **marvelous. My soul knows you are marvelous.**

Wars Fought and Won

Daughter,

There is much shifting going on in the spirit realm. Wars are being fought and won by my Spirit. As victories are secured in that realm, victories will begin to filter down into the natural realm. My angels are fighting for my children. I am happy to give victory to them.

Continue to stand and believe in me and in my words. This is not the time to fold up your tent and go home.

I will deal with those that have harmed your soul, at the same time applying healing salve upon your wounds. Stand still and allow me to check you out from head to toe. I believe I have been called "The Great Physician." I have many years of practice and know just what to do for my children to cause a speedy recovery.

It is difficult for my children to imagine an abundant life, a life free of pain and concern, but there is a place in me where all striving ceases. It is a resting-place that I have provided for my believing ones. Come on into my place of healing and safety. You are welcome to enter in.

Keep your options open, stay pliable in my hands. I am shaping you into my design. Each design I create is unique in every way.

I have special things I desire to accomplish in each life, do not fight the process. Just as the clay is applied to the potter's wheel and offers no resistance to change, so you too must relax and allow me to shape and make you into a beautiful vessel, one that pleases me. I will place the finished product on a stage for all to see.

Father

Dear Father,

I thank you that your power far exceeds the power of the enemy. I thank you that victories are being won by your Spirit every moment of every day. As I awaken each morning I look for results to appear in the areas of war where I have believed for your victory.

Your angels fight every day to bring answers to the prayers of your children; I am one that will reap the benefits of the angel's successes in battle.

I continue to stand in faith that you answer my prayers. I believe the promises you have made to me; I won't give up and quit.

Your healing salve is what I need for the battle wounds, thank you for applying it liberally to the injured areas. I know you as my "Great Physician"; you know exactly what is wrong and how to bring a quick fix.

I release those that have harmed me, and place them in your hands. You will do what is best in these situations.

Father, I want to enter this place where all striving ceases, show me how. I need your resting place; I want your healing and safety in my life.

Father, I remain pliable in your hands; make me into your image.

Thank you that I am wondrously made by your hands. I yield to the work you wish to do in my life; I want to be like the clay that offers no resistance to your shaping.

When I look into a mirror, I want to see your reflection.

In Jesus' name I pray,

Your Work In Progress

> **Psalms 139: 15 – 18   My substance was not hidden from you when I was made in secret in my mother's womb.   Your eyes saw me there, even before. You wrote about me before I was created. How precious are the thoughts you had of me? How great is the total of your thoughts of me! If I could count your thoughts of me, they would outnumber the sand.**

Anxiety

Daughter,

This morning My Spirit is busy working anxiety out of your life. He is working on you with spiritual "scrubbing bubbles". I am removing the residue of your fears. Fear has torment, and that is the last thing I want for your life.

Now let me do a final wash and then my love will rinse the hurt and pain away, just as I washed away all of your sins. Sometimes it seems there is no remedy to a problem you face, but there is always a solution. It may be around the problem, over it, or under it…and sometimes the best way, the shortest route, is by simply moving straight through the problem.

The fire from this fiery furnace looks and feels like it will burn you alive, but your trust grows as you see no flames on your body and no smell of smoke upon your garments. I bring my children through the furnace of afflictions.

Keep moving; don't stop. There are steps on the other side by which you may climb to safety.

I see the stress operating in your soul, but the pressure will be relieved. My angels have already been summonsed to bring relief to your suffering. My power will break this thing and you will be set free. You will be like a bird set free from a snare.

Father

Dear Father,

I thank you for your cleaning supplies that remove every last bit of residue from the abuse inflicted upon me by the thief.

Anxiety and fear is not what I want either. I submit myself for your inspection and receive a total healing of all pain and hurts of the past.

Lord, I know that you know the best way out of my troubles, so I give you my hand and ask that your hand lead me to a place of safety.

You are right, Lord. Even though I thought the enemy was going to swallow me alive, I am here in your presence, alive. My body is burn free, and there is no residue of smoke on my garments. You keep your children when they go through the furnace of afflictions.

I won't stop Lord, I'm moving … I see the exit stairs from here. Thank you for relieving all stress and strain. You are a caring Father.

I receive your release from the enemy's snare, and I'm chirping like a bird for the joy of my salvation.

In Jesus' name I pray,

Your Chirpy Daughter

> **Psalms 140:12   I know that the Lord will maintain the cause of the afflicted and the rights of the poor.**

Returning

Daughter,

Today I have returned family relationships to you. The Spirit proclaims this. The barriers erected by the enemy will be torn down, and once again your family will be whole.

They will return in the order I have shown you, nothing is too hard for me. Praise me for doing this for you.

Prepare your heart for deeper revelation. I will speak to you in the night season and you shall cry aloud the Word of the Sovereign Lord in the daytime.

Visions and dreams will increase; my power will pour through your body as you stretch out your hands to the hurting, poor, and needy.

I will make your life so full that you will not miss the companionship of a mate. I will enrich you with new friends, ones who will cheer you to run your race to win. I will send you ones who will hold up your arms in prayer.

They will be used by me to cut through the jungle of delays and detours, the things being used by the enemy to try neutralizing your contributions in the war against crime! The enemy is a master criminal; he is the original con artist, draped in cloaks of deceit and destruction.

However he has a gigantic problem … His major problem is me! -- I hold a superior rank: King of Kings, Lord of Lords, Commander of the Lord's Host is my Name! He has been stripped of everything he counted on, and now all he can do is look for an innocent that he can bully into submission.

He met his match in me, and he will soon be no more.

Father

Dear King of Kings,

You desire that your children believe what you say regardless of the things they see, feel, or hear. My heart is thrilled that you have promised me a closer relationship with the family that you have given to me. The enemy never wins, but he keeps trying, and I wonder why he doesn't get the picture.

Thank you for the times that you pull me aside and speak words of comfort and revelation. I will speak those things that you whisper in my ears.

Thank you for my close golden friends and for the new ones too. Their prayers and friendships are greatly appreciated. Through our prayers, the enemy will be turned back, disgraced in battle.

Father, I thank you that you are my problem solver. I thank you for your superior power over the enemy.

In Jesus' name I pray,

Your Prepared Daughter

Psalms 144:15	Happy are the people whose God is the Lord!

Feelings Are Not to Be Trusted

Daughter,

Tonight you are feeling about as useless as a hood ornament on a vehicle. Why do you feel like that?

I have called you, anointed you, and used you for my honor and my glory. May I share with you the reason you are feeling this way? It is because things have unfolded in a way you have not envisioned.

I am bigger than life or its circumstances, and can order change at any moment of your life. Give me all of your cares and burdens. Stress causes your heart to be heavy laden and full of cares. Trust me to take care of you. You cannot work it out yourself; it is by grace that I move in your life.

As you study the book of Acts, notice my hand selecting, by my choice, who I will use, and who I will bless.

Line up for your blessings, you have many on the way.

A special hedge of protection surrounds your family; they are also blessed because of my hand upon you.

I am positioning you to work for me in my fields that I have called you to. The enemy is mad, but no matter of this, he is defeated. Be my giant slayer. I will go before you and build the ministry. The words of the naysayers will be put to nothing, they will evaporate into thin air. I have the final say on what goes on in your life.

Stand up straight and tall, let me decorate you with my ribbons for distinguished service. I have one for valor under fire, for bravery in your own war, and ribbons for helping rescue your brethren.

I'll even give you a parade. You know the kind I like... the parade with all evil spirits held captive at the end of the procession!

As you pour out your heart to me, I will set things right. You are a little shell shocked right now, but much life will come shining through to you. The battle is nearly over and the tide is turning.

Do not be entangled with people who would put you in bondage to their ideas for your life. I like being in charge of you and will help you to understand what I want of your life.

For now, just relax and take one day at a time.

Omnipotent Father

Omnipotent Father,

Forgive me for forgetting how much you have done in my life, and all of the things that you have given to me.

I thank you that you are bigger than anything that is going on in my life, and you can order change at a moments notice.

Help me to understand what is going on around me, give me your understanding. Thank you for your grace added to my life. I am standing in line awaiting the blessings you have spoken to me about. Thank you for the hedge of protection that surrounds my family and me.

You have a special place for me to work in your fields, so regardless of the anger of those around me, I will do as instructed by your Spirit.

I love it when you confound those that think they know what is best for people, you are the only one knowing the ending from the beginning. I am humbled by the commendations for working in the service of my Commander in Chief.

Regardless of how I feel, I know you will set things right in my life, my trust is in you. Thank you that the tide of the battle has already begun to turn in my favor. Father, I ask you for wisdom in choosing friends and acquaintances, you know the heart of man, so I ask for your help in my choices. I am relaxed in you Lord, and enjoying one day at a time.

In Jesus' name I pray,

Your Chosen Vessel

Psalms 145: 17 -20 The Lord is righteous in all His works. The Lord is near to those who call upon him in truth. He will fulfill the desire of those who fear Him; he will hear their cry and save them. The Lord preserves those who love Him.

Walking With Me

Daughter,

Walking with me can be exciting and rewarding. It can be dangerous as well. There are attacks along the way, but my Spirit is stronger than any attack the enemy can throw at you.

Others may think they know what is best for your life, but it is only I that can see around every bend in the road. I want a prosperous journey for you. Listen to my advice and counsel. I will give you my very best.

You cannot build your own ministry. It is my ministry in you. I will do what is good for your life. Trust is absolutely required in this walk I have called you to.

Do not expect others to understand the way I am taking you. I will confirm my leading to you.

Off now, the journey continues! Don't allow the enemy to push you in your mind. Enjoy the life I have given you. I will control its outcome. Just let go and enjoy me, for I want to make you happy.

Father

Dear Father,

I want to thank you that your Spirit is stronger than any attack launched against my life. You alone know what is good for me, and I trust you with all of my heart to do what is best.

My ears are listening to your counsel and advice; I can depend upon the love you have for me. Father thank you for an exciting and rewarding life, I am walking each day with expectation of the prosperity you have promised.

I refuse to allow the enemy to push me around; I push him in Jesus' name. Father, you are in control of my life, and I can trust you for blessings every day.

Thank you for wanting only the best things for my life.

In Jesus' name I pray,

Your Rewarded Daughter

> **Psalms 147:1   Praise the Lord for it is good to sing praises to our God.**

Grow Your Faith

Daughter,

While you are "in the waiting," allow this perfect opportunity to grow your faith. First, a trust relationship is established. Then love for my faithfulness grows and blossoms in this type of soil. This soil I speak of is one produced by trust.

Hold out your hand to me and I will give you manna straight from my throne. You have yet to taste of all of my goodness. Eat your fill, I have plenty to spare.

Your heart is beating as my heart. I too want my people encouraged, healed and set free. I have given you my heart and I am anointing your words with great power and authority.

You have passed this most recent test; it was with the help of your friend, Jesus. You were not aware that this was a test, but by this you have been sanded and refined.

Crying is ceasing. Let me prove myself faithful to you. I will always lovingly care for you. Do not worry about what will become of you, I have your life in my hands. As long as you obey my instructions, a wonderful way will be made for you.

Father

Father,

Thank you for this time of growth. I will not lie to you, no one can. It has been hard on me to wait, not knowing. Here is my hand Lord, thank you for good things to taste of. I desire everything you have for me.

Thank you for sharing with me your heart, I welcome the anointing of the Holy Spirit I open my heart to you. Fill me up.

You have lovingly cared for me; I will cease from crying and worrying about the future, for you are my future.

My desire is to please you in every moment of my life.

In Jesus' name I pray.

Your Refined Daughter

> Psalms 147:11 The Lord takes pleasure in those who fear Him, in those who hope in His mercy.

The Anointing

Daughter,

You are anxious to speak with me tonight because of the anointing you felt that was swirling deep within. I want you stirred; new life is good for you. I want to see the return of my sparkly woman of God.

I am blowing my breath upon you; cobwebs of the past are vanishing.

Listen carefully to my instructions. I am speaking now and volume will increase and be repeated from several different directions, showing to you that I indeed am pointing out the way you are to go.

I want you to be sure and steadfast about your decisions. When that is not so, the mind will wander from yes to no, and no to yes, just as a wave of the sea goes in and then back out. I want this thing set in stone for you. When in doubt, "don't,"... Not anything... wait and pray.

Others will try advising, they are well meaning, but none can see the total picture as I can. They limit me, one who has no limits. I am getting you ready for a new adventure. No one can hold you down for it is I who launches you!

Some miss all I can do for them because of refusal to listen and follow my instructions. They strive to serve me well, yet refuse my Spirit to rule and reign in their decisions.

My children can't chase rainbows; have you have heard of "fools gold?" This is what they find chasing after when they chase things that simply glitter. Go after the real thing, go with divine instruction.

Sit at my feet until you get my counsel – it will be worth the wait. The clock is ticking, and each person must run their race at the speed I set for them.

Listening and obeying can bring wonderful results.

Father

Dear Father,

Thank you for your anointing, for the new life I feel stirring within me. I am so glad that you desire my life to be filled with good things, this thrills my soul, and I am happy in you.

Thank you for the new breath of the Holy Spirit that is now blowing upon my life. My ears are listening to hear your directions, thank you for the increase of your anointing.

Thank you for definite, clear instructions, I will only move when you speak a definite yes to my spirit. I no longer go to others for their opinions; I come to you because you know everything. It is wonderful to know that you have no limits.

Thank you for the new adventure that you are speaking to me about, thank you for the launch.

It is my desire to hear your voice, and follow your instructions to the letter. Help me to do this, Father.

No more rainbow chasing for me, fool's gold can't buy anything of value. I am going for the real deal, the real gold, those promises of God that bring lasting wealth and happiness.

Here at your feet I sit, Lord. Speak your words of counsel to a daughter who desires your will in her life.

If I am running too slow, speed me up, and if I am moving too fast, rein me in. Thank you for the wonderful results in serving you.

In Jesus' name I pray,

Your Sparkly Daughter

Psalms 148:5 Let them praise the name of the LORD; for he commanded and they were created.

Plentiful Grace

Dear Daughter,

You have a major situation that is troubling you immensely. I know you would like to see me move in the twinkling of an eye. I have waited many long years for you to grow and mature, now you must give me the necessary time needed to create change with this issue.

I have plentiful grace for you until this is all worked out. Receive my grace every moment of the day and night. Daughter, there are so many ways that you are pleasing me, but wanting to serve me is at the top of the list.

It is now time to go. You may feel a little numb in the beginning. It will like going from the idle position, to the Indy 500! It's going to be quick, so get your mind ready for sudden movement.

I want to see my laughing little girl again; be happy and fulfilled. Give it your best, and I'll be beside you all of the way.

Father

Dear Father,

I thank you that you see what I am facing in life. I relax now and place this in your hands, and you will move to correct this problem.

Thank you for grace to walk through this period of my life, and I receive grace every morning and every evening for this hurtful situation.

Thank you for noticing that I do sincerely want to serve you.

Wow Lord, I've never been to the races. Thank you for the acceleration in my life; help me get my mind ready for the race. From idle to the Indy 500…what a trip that will be. I thank you, Father.

Thank you for desiring good things for my life, no other Father could care so well for my life.

By the grace of God, I will do my best, thank you for staying right by my side.

In Jesus' name I pray,

Your Indy Driver

Psalms 149:4 The LORD takes pleasure in his people.

Sin-Sick World

Daughter,

You live in a crazy, sin-sick world, decay is all around. This is proof to you that the hour is late and darkness is settling upon the land. Remember that darkness is as light to me and I can still rescue and deliver by my great power.

I have summonsed you as my representative to carry my light into the dark places of the world. The words I shall give you will confound the wise. My anointing will reside upon your speech, music, and gifting in the realm of the supernatural.

I will not send you broken and spilled out. I will restore you to perfect health and then, on your way! I will take you at your word that you will go for me. I value greatly the words that flow from your mouth. Be not concerned when things shift and change in your life, because I am always in charge.

Change can be good, look for the silver lining in this period of your life, there is one. I intend to bless and keep you safe, secure, and happy. I have listened to the cry of your heart and I am here to answer and attend to all of your needs.

I have not forgotten my promise of material things and finances you need for your life and for your work. You will have surprising field trips and be in the spotlight as you carry out my work.

Father

Father,

You have shown to me the lateness of the hour. You have said for us to work while it is still day, so, Father, send your children on assignments for you.

I believe there are no hard cases with you, deliverance can come to the big cases as well as the small ones, as you begin to deliver people in trouble.

Thank you for the call of God upon my life. I thank you for the anointing of the Holy Spirit that has been placed there.

I receive your healing for the hurts and broken placed of my heart and soul. I need your touch so I can run the race set before me with a fullness of your power.

Thank you that you are in charge of me. Everything that flows into my life has been filtered by your hand.

It is wonderful to be in a family where the Father keeps me safe, happy, and secure. Thank you for hearing my cries, and for hearing and answering my prayers.

I thank you that you keep every promise you make, for you are not a promise breaker, but you are a promise keeper.

I have made all of my requests known to you for you are the only one that can truly help and deliver me.

In Jesus' name I pray,

You Safe, Secure, and Happy Daughter

Psalms 146:8 The LORD opens the eyes of the blind and raises those who are bowed down. The LORD loves the righteous.

The Importance of Prayer

Daughter,

You are beginning to get the picture about the possibility that your call may develop in a different arena and format that you first thought. Many of my generals suffered through things that were unnecessary by not understanding how their gifting was to be developed. Just let it all go tonight and let me make your life good.

Do not look upon this minor setback as an ending, but as a new beginning into the places I shall carry you.

What I am stressing to you right now is the importance of prayer before decisions are made. Do not move unless I show you that it of me.

I want to reveal my will to you and will do so as you seek my face. Let me cast the deciding vote on all decisions. Leave nothing to chance!

You have been on the potter's wheel and I have caused some changes in you. Now that this is accomplished, I will now start adding more blessings into your life. Love me, love my people. Keep in touch...

Just as I spoke to you regarding my will for you to remain in a secluded place, I will continue to reveal my will for you in every area of your life. More direction is coming, so stay quiet before me. I need quiet around you to finish this last touch upon the preparation for your night with your King. Out of this encounter with me, the world will be blessed.

Promotion is coming to you. The ways of my Spirit will be further revealed to you. Do not fear the future. I know every day of your life from the beginning on, and I have all things in my control.

Father

Father,

I thank you for revelation knowledge from you. I want your thoughts and directions in every decision I make. Today I release all of the things that are giving me aggravation and concerns and I am looking to you for the good life that you have promised.

Thank you for the wisdom you have given to me that I should always pray before doing anything. This will keep me out of a lot of trouble. I want to stay in constant touch with you; I can't make it without your help.

In this quiet time I am hearing more direction for my life, thank you for turning up the volume and for quieting my mind so that I can hear you.

Thank you for preparing me for the new things that you have for me.

I reject fear of all kind, in the name of Jesus, and trust you with all of my heart.

In Jesus' name I pray,

Your Prayerful Daughter

Psalms 147:5 Great is our LORD, and great is His power. His understanding is infinite.

I Re-lit Your Torch

Daughter,

I have re-lit your torch. Go for me in my power. Begin to say that everything that was stolen must be given back. The bully will have no choice but, to give it up!

Many surprises will come back to you. I have instructed you in this thing because I have decreed it is time for change and restoration. I want you to become more aggressive in the Spirit. I will back you up. Speak out!

There are two categories that the world describes as the "haves and the have nots."

I prefer you in the former, not the latter. You understand, I am not only speaking of what you possess, I am also speaking of the true riches of my Kingdom where I desire you live.

I get no glory when you are bombarded with loss. I am the repairer of the breach, the broken walls where the enemy enters into your life.

I will only allow you to submit to a leadership that is in accordance with my plan for your life. Some have forfeited their place in your life because of leading contrary to my will for you. There are times when the baton must be passed, and I once again will stand in that role.

I will not allow you to be abused. My little one, you are worth more to me than that. Crumbs and morsels are not enough for you. I want to give you more; I do have more for you. Let me bless you. You are my beloved and I am yours!

I will take care of the shame and the embarrassment. I will hide you from the wagging tongues; I will cause their tongues to stick to the roof of their mouth.

                                                            Father

Dear Father,

I thank you for touching my life again. I will go in your power and authority. Everything that has been stolen from me must be returned in Jesus' name.

Give it up, you enemy of God!

I am obedient to say with my mouth what I want, and not saying what I now have. Thank you Lord that it is your will for me to prosper, I believe you give to me the true riches of your kingdom, and financial blessings for my needs as well.

Thank you for being to me a repairer of the breach in my life. When you finish, I am better than new.

I submit to your leadership, I also submit to those in authority over me as commanded in your Word.

Thank you for commanding an end of abuse of all kinds, for in your eyes I have great value.

I have moved my chair to your table where I belong, and someone else can have the crumbs...this is my time to be blessed. I thank you that we belong together.

Thank you for removing all shame and embarrassment. Your dealings have now come to those with wagging tongues.

In Jesus' name I pray,

Your Little Daughter

Psalms 147:5 He heals the brokenhearted and heals their wounds.

While It Is Day

Daughter,

You must work while it is still day. Prepare to move out into your calling. You were prepared for such a time as this. The enemy has known your needs and your weaknesses. He has played his game to hurt you. However, you are not dead yet and I say as I have said before, "Can These Bones Live?"

Well dear, the bones are rattling, coming together, muscle and sinews being applied and a new you is coming forth, basking in the power of a living God! You will hardly recognize yourself. A new woman is being created. I am beginning to heal your tender joints, your aches, and your pains. My angel has my healing oil for you, and it will be applied routinely. Even vehicles have need of maintenance. You are in need of a going over and I am going to do this for you. The pain will leave your body; you will be strengthened and made just like new.

I have spoken to you that my angels carry what you need, and I have released my word for your healing. There is much more I will do for your body, you will say, "it feels so good to be healthy again." I will give you a keen appreciation for a pain free body. As my healing anointing flows through you to others, it will also find its way into the needy areas of your body.

Your entire family will be blessed because of you. Special blessings will be released to that those who reached out to you in your time of need. I know what will bring joy and happiness and that is what I give.

I have given you hope again. Nothing in the natural has happened. Your circumstances haven't changed yet, but I have changed you. Your focus has shifted, you now are looking at what can be, not what is. That is true faith!

Lovingly,
Mighty God, Your Father

Dear Mighty God, My Father,

I am prepared to be a vessel that you can flow through. Thank you for healing me, for bringing new life back into my life. I thank you for a pain free body and mind.

Your angels are so awesome, thank you for all that you give them to do for me.

Father, I thank you that as I trust and obey you, others dear to me are blessed by you.

I receive the new hope that has been placed within my heart; thank you. I walk by faith and not by sight. You are doing everything that you have promised; you do not lie, or promise things you won't deliver.

I stand and await your promises to me, thanking you and blessing your Holy Name. Thank you for changing me, for molding me into your image.

I am looking at what you have said will be and not gazing upon what the circumstances are saying. Circumstances must move to make room for my Father, he is Almighty God!

In Jesus' name I pray,

Blessed,
Your Pain-Free Daughter

Psalms 147:6 The LORD lifts up the meek and throws the wicked down.

You Arrived Alive!

Daughter,

You have arrived alive, and I am still keeping you. Stretch to look into the realm of the Holy Spirit, for He can show many examples of my love and care for you.

When things seem at their very worst is when I move quickly and turn everything around. Rest your weary mind, I will not fail to care for you, use your faith and let's get everything turned around.

Why were you discouraged and cast down today? You may not realize it, but you are in the center of a great miracle. One day can change your entire future.

Trust me for that one day. Have you heard of my"suddenlies?"

The enemy has been hammering you about your age. I can produce fruit at any age. Do you remember Sarah? I said you would produce fruit in your latter years. I am working for you. Do not be distracted by the whispers of the enemy.

It has not escaped my notice that the road has been rough, but I bring good news to you today that things are now ready, and you will experience a better life.

Hold to my promises for a moment longer. The miracles are in sight!

Good night, my little warrior. I am guiding you.

Watchful Father

Dear Watchful Father,

I thank you for keeping me. The journey has been rough. Thank you, God, I am still breathing after the violent attacks upon my soul.

I now stretch to see every example of your love and care for me. Lord, you have turned even the bad things that have happened and made them good.

Nothing is impossible with you. You defeated this enemy and brought amazing results to the Glory of God. Thank you for total deliverance.

I refuse to be discouraged or defeated. Circumstances are just that, circumstances. You are Mighty God. You have changed circumstances in the blink of an eye. You arrived fully armed and wiped out the enemy.

It is nice to know that I am in the center of a miracle. I see it, I feel it. I am witness to it. You have said it, so it's settled. Thank you.

I love suddenlies! They are so thrilling.

Thank you that your children come in all sizes, colors, young and old alike. You work in all of us; you are the one who is faithful.

Thank you for the miracles, Thank you for permanence.

In Jesus' name I pray and worship you with a thankful heart,

Triumphantly,
Your Little Warrior

Psalms 21:2   You, LORD, have given me my heart's desire, and have not withheld the request of my lips.

www.ingramcontent.com/pod-product-compliance
Lightning Source LLC
Chambersburg PA
CBHW072002040426
42447CB00009B/1444